CLOSING THE ACHIEVEMENT GAP

A Vision for
Changing Beliefs
and Practices

Edited by Belinda Williams

Association for Supervision and Curriculum Development
Alexandria, Virginia

Association for Supervision and Curriculum Development
1250 N. Pitt St., Alexandria, Virginia 22314-1453
Telephone: (800)933-2723 or (703)549-9110. Fax: (703)299-8631

Gene R. Carter, *Executive Director*
Michelle Terry, *Assistant Executive Director, Program Development*
Ronald S. Brandt, *Assistant Executive Director*
Nancy Modrak, *Managing Editor, ASCD Books*
Darcie Simpson, *Associate Editor*
René Bahrenfuss, *Copyeditor*
Maritza Bourque, *Project Assistant*
Gary Bloom, *Manager, Design and Production Services*
Karen Monaco, *Designer*
Tracey A. Smith, *Production Coordinator*
Dina Murray, *Production Assistant*
Valerie Sprague, *Desktop Publisher*

Development of some of the material in this book was supported in part by the U.S. Department of Education, Office of Educational Research and Improvement, under contract numbers RP9 1002001 through RP9 1002010. The content of this publication does not necessarily reflect the views of any individual laboratory, the Department of Education, or any other agency of the U.S. Government.

ASCD publications present a variety of viewpoints. The views expressed or implied in this book should not be interpreted as official positions of the Association.

Printed in the United States of America.

ASCD Stock No. 196227
s10/96
Prices: ASCD Members, $16.95; Nonmembers, $20.95

Library of Congress Cataloging-in-Publication Data
Closing the achievement gap : a vision for changing beliefs and
    practices / edited by Belinda Williams.
        p.   cm.
    Includes bibliographical references.
    ISBN 0-87120-273-5
    1. Education, Urban—Social aspects—United States. 2. Socially
handicapped children—Education—United States. 3. Educational
equalization—United States. 4. Academic achievement—United
States. I. Williams, Belinda.
    LC5131.C56 1996 370'.91732—dc20   96-35607
                                                   CIP

00 99 98 97 96   5 4 3 2 1

CLOSING THE ACHIEVEMENT GAP: A VISION FOR CHANGING BELIEFS AND PRACTICES

Preface

During the nearly three decades since their inception, the Regional Educational Laboratories, funded by the Office of Educational Research and Improvement of the U.S. Department of Education, have proven to be valuable resources. Each Laboratory identifies regional needs and develops resources to help meet them. In cooperation with partners in state and intermediate education agencies, universities, professional associations, foundations, businesses, and other social service agencies, the laboratories provide programs and services to schools and others working to improve education.

In 1992, the Regional Educational Laboratory Network was established in recognition of the growing need for coordinated national responses to educational challenges in the United States—and the potential of Laboratories working collaboratively to help meet this need. All 10 have joined together to formalize, consolidate, and extend their capability to act as a national system.

The structure for achieving this goal is a set of collaborative projects, staffed and supported by all or a subset of the Regional Laboratories. Each project has an originating (or "lead") Laboratory that provides a project coordinator. The coordinator forms a steering committee (called the design team) to shape the project plan and activities. Collaborating Laboratories then provide one or more staff members, usually part-time, to help carry out the project.

THE URBAN EDUCATION NATIONAL NETWORK

To support the restructuring efforts of the nation's urban school districts, the Urban Education National Network (UENN) was established in 1993 to consolidate the knowledge base in urban education and bring focus to the expertise and resources in urban education that exist in the Regional Laboratories. A central role of the network is to provide information and assistance to educators as they work to increase the academic performance of urban students whose traditions and experiences are not adequately represented within the current educational system. The UENN Task Force also seeks to contribute to present reform proposals and activities being carried out at both the national and local community levels.

Disturbing numbers of poor and minority students in U.S. urban schools continue to underachieve academically. In spite of years of reform, a persistent achievement gap remains between students in urban schools and elsewhere. Many practitioners and policymakers agree that this situation cannot persist; urban students must be given the caliber of education they need to fully contribute to a democratic society. Simply stating the goal of "higher achievement for all students" isn't enough. In order to transform U.S. schools, we need to impart knowledge about what works best in the urban context and provide ongoing support for reform efforts.

A groundswell of activity on behalf of urban learners and their schools is being generated at the local level. Parents, citizens, educators, and businesspeople are mobilizing to redesign educational and human development organizations to better serve urban children and their families through a system of integrated services. Much of this activity has grown out of recent efforts by urban districts to decentralize bureaucracies that have often impeded change and innovation at the local school level. Additional activity has resulted from reform efforts taking place in other social service agencies serving urban children and their families.

The movement toward integrated services is but one of the newer conceptualizations of student development, the teaching-learning process, and educational groups that are convening to support the restructuring of urban school districts. Conventional educational approaches are being altered, in some places radically, to prepare urban schools and teachers to educate students of the 21st century.

The chapters in this book have been commissioned by the UENN to:

• Define the nature of obstacles to urban academic performance. We must clarify deterrents to the development of urban lifelong learners, such as the lack of curriculum relevance and authenticity, and describe supportive environments, appropriate staff development, and meaningful instruction and assessments for urban students.

• Identify, validate, and disseminate a knowledge base of theory and practice that will better inform decision making relevant to overcoming these performance obstacles.

In addition to the authors' important work, this book represents many hours of discussion and efforts on the part of the members of the Urban Education National Network Task Force. The Task Force identified the broad issues and bodies of research that should be considered in developing this book. In addition, Ellen Newcombe, Research Associate, Research for Better Schools (RBS), put aside other important responsibilities to make valuable contributions to the book's review and development. Grateful appreciation is also extended to Diane Rosen, Support Specialist (RBS), for providing many hours of helpful editorial assistance and typing manuscripts.

TASK FORCE MEMBERS: URBAN EDUCATION NATIONAL NETWORK*

Lisa Carlos, *Senior Policy Analyst*
Far West Laboratory for Educational Research and Development (FWL)

Loyce Caruthers, *Senior Program Associate*
Mid-Continent Regional Educational Laboratory (McREL)

Deborah Childs-Bowen, *Director of Field Services*
SouthEastern Regional Vision for Education (SERVE)

Efrain Fuentes, *Staff Associate*
The Regional Laboratory for Educational Improvement of the Northeast and Islands (NE&I)

Patricia Guerra, *Research Associate*
Southwest Educational Development Laboratory (SEDL)

Deborah V. Jolly, *Vice President, Services for School Improvement*
Southwest Educational Development Laboratory (SEDL)

Patricia S. Kusimo, *Director of Education Services Program*
Appalachia Educational Laboratory (AEL)

Robin LaSota, *Program Coordinator, Urban Education*
North Central Regional Educational Laboratory (NCREL)

Ethel Simon-McWilliams, *Associate Executive Director*
Northwest Regional Educational Laboratory (NWREL)

Lynn J. Stinnette, *Director, Urban Education*
North Central Regional Educational Laboratory (NCREL)

Belinda Williams, *Director, Urban Education Project*
Research for Better Schools (RBS)

Leadership provided by Stinnette and Williams.

*Editor's note
The UENN was established by the U.S. Department of Education, Office of Educational Research and Improvement Regional Educational Laboratories during the 1990–95 contract period. As a result of the 1996–2000 contract awards, the following clarification is needed:

1. The UENN no longer exists.

2. The UENN members are listed with their laboratory affiliation at the time this book was developed. A current list of Regional Educational Laboratories is in the Appendix.

3. The Task Force is the same as the UENN. The members were the lab representatives to the UENN.

1

The Nature of the Achievement Gap: The Call for a Vision to Guide Change

BELINDA WILLIAMS

S tudents from poor and minority groups face a very un-
certain time in U.S. education. Their economic and social
conditions are deteriorating without relief in sight, and
the progressive curriculum reforms, if carried out one school
at a time, will almost certainly place them at an even greater
disadvantage. . . . Our gravest concern is whether there is sufficient commitment in our society to significantly and directly
address the problems of educational equity through any sus-
tained and coherent strategy. . . . [The] vision of change must
be powerful enough to focus the public and all the levels of
the governance system on common challenging purposes and
to sustain that focus over an extended period of time (O'Day
and Smith 1993, pp. 267, 298-299).

The vision and commitment to change that O'Day and Smith es-
pouse should alert everyone in our society to the severity of conditions in urban schools. This book defines that vision and commitment

further. It synthesizes research and theory on urban communities, schools, and students for decision makers at all levels who are responsible for policy, funding, research, community and family support, and education.

Four major themes run through the research and theory presented here:

• Calls for paradigm shifts in understanding the role of social interaction, values, and standards in human development in urban contexts.

• Caution against views of intervention in urban schools that reduce the focus to curriculum, instruction, and assessment.

• Challenges to current deficit and at-risk characterizations of poor urban students.

• Reconceptualizations of teacher preparation along with support for organizational change in schools and classrooms.

Many political, economic, social, and technological forces are pressuring schools to restructure so that they serve all students better. There is significant evidence, however, that generic restructuring frameworks and designs will not change urban schools. The generic frameworks and designs do not pay sufficient attention to the unique issues and conditions that these schools must confront every day (Lytle 1992, Newmann 1993, Passow 1992, Urban Education Project 1994, Williams and Newcombe 1994).

Still, many educators continue to seek the single approach to "good teaching" that will improve all students' achievement (Haberman 1991). They attribute urban students' low academic achievement to their lack of ability, "culture," and motivation to learn. The Commission on Chapter 1 (1992) explained the situation this way:

> Most Americans assume that the low achievement of poor and minority children is bound up in the children themselves or their families. "The children don't try." "They have no place to study. . . . Their parents don't care." "Their culture does not value education." These and other excuses are regularly offered up to explain the achievement gap that separates poor and minority students from other young Americans (p. 3).

Urban schools, as Jonathan Kozol (1991) so vividly described them in *Savage Inequalities*, face great challenges. In a recent Council of the Great City Schools survey (1994), urban superintendents, school board members, and school administrators—together responsible for 5.4 million students, 7,392 schools, and budgets totaling $31.8 billion—identified violence and gang-related activity, the lack of parent involvement, and bilingual education and non-English speaking students as their three most pressing problems. Academic achievement ranked 8th in their top 10 issues. Among the other issues were buildings that need repair and renovation, increasing poverty, budget constraints, an influx of immigrants, drug use, a shrinking middle-class tax base, and declining job opportunities (Ottinger and Root 1994). Urban demographic predictions (Hodgekinson 1985, O'Day and Smith 1993) indicate that these challenges are likely to increase.

We believe that the greatest challenge for urban schools is the issue of low academic achievement. A recent report, *Making Schools Work for Children in Poverty* (Commission on Chapter 1 1992), concludes that low expectations and the absence of rigor in urban schools with concentrations of children in poverty "consigns them to lives without the knowledge and skills they need to exist anywhere but on the margins of our society and consigns the rest of us to forever bear the burden of their support" (p. 3). In addition, a review of 100 studies of academic performance and delinquency involving more than 30,000 students establishes that students who receive average grades of *D*'s or *F*'s are 2.1 times more likely to be delinquent (involved in violating laws) than their peers who receive grades of *C* or better (Maguin 1994).

What do research and theory recommend to improve urban students' achievement? Where should change begin? Who is responsible? Any analysis of urban education with a view toward change must begin by identifying both historical and contemporary socioeconomic dynamics that contribute to the unique characteristics of urban communities, schools, and students. The combined effects of concentrated poverty, cultural diversity, and isolation of urban neighborhoods according to race, ethnicity, and socioeconomic status are central to that analysis (Yancey and Saporito 1994). It is equally important to examine the ways in which the concentration of poverty and cultural diversity are linked to the economic history of the

United States and the ecological relationship between economic development and opportunity structures.

Bartelt (1994), citing Bluestone and Harrison (1982) and O'Connor (1973), identifies three macrosocial forces that have shaped economic development and opportunity structures in cities:

• the growth of suburbs and the relocation of manufacturing,

• the segregation of less economically viable populations by poverty and race, and

• the growth of a postindustrial service economy that requires different job skills and so affects employment possibilities and cities' tax bases.

Bartelt (1994) concludes, "[I]nner city schools are increasingly the schools of remnant populations and communities trapped by their economic irrelevance or their links to diminished labor markets."

These macrosocial forces reflect, and are further complicated by, two historical dynamics: the racial segregation of public school education and the immigration of Hispanic and other ethnic and linguistic minority populations to the United States. Forty years after *Brown v. Board of Education of Topeka, Kansas*, the U.S. Supreme Court's decision declaring de jure racial segregation of schools unconstitutional, and 30 years after the 1964 Civil Rights Act mandated school integration, integration in this country is declining (Brown 1994, Orfield 1994). The failure of both the *Brown* decision and the 1964 Civil Rights Act to effectively bring about school desegregation is one of the primary causes for the racial isolation of large numbers of black and Hispanic students in urban schools. In a 1994 report of the Harvard Project on School Desegregation to the National School Boards Association, Orfield establishes the relationship of segregation to poverty. In addition, he states:

> Latino students will soon be the largest minority group in the U.S. public schools. . . . [B]oth African-American and Latino students are much more likely than white students to find themselves in schools of concentrated poverty . . . [;] much of the education damage of racial segregation grows out of this relationship . . . . [S]egregation remains high in big cities and serious in mid-sized central cities (Orfield 1994, p. 1).

Against such a backdrop, what can urban communities and schools do to improve the formal education that they provide? How can they prepare urban students to enter the job market, contribute to society, and achieve a satisfying quality of life?

A number of efforts have been made. Since enactment of the Chapter 1 program in 1965, the federal government has distributed more than $70 billion to pay for extra basic skills instruction in schools with concentrations of poor children. As a result of these additional services, the achievement gap separating poor and minority students from more advantaged students declined by nearly half (Commission on Chapter 1 1992).

While Chapter 1 has paid off in decreasing the achievement gap between poor children and their advantaged peers in basic skills, Chapter 1 programs do not develop the ability to analyze and communicate complex ideas, both of which are requirements for securing positions in an increasingly technological society. Assuring that poor children and children of color in urban schools receive a real education, with the supports they need for learning, requires us to challenge widespread assumptions about their learning ability and about educational reform (Astuto, Clark, Read, McGree, and Fernandez 1993; Urban Education Project 1994; Williams and Newcombe 1994).

Astuto and colleagues (1993, pp. 133-134) identify the following assumptions as having specific implications for urban reform efforts, and they suggest alternatives.

Current Assumptions	**Alternatives**
Achievement in school rests predominantly in the hands of the individual student.	Individual achievement in school is influenced markedly by the adjustment of the school to the student client.
Schools can effect only marginal, value-added gain in the education of students from differing economic and cultural backgrounds.	Schools can interrupt the deterministic relationship of educational performance and socioeconomic status through in-school interventions.
Schooling supports and promotes a common cultural heritage.	Schooling supports and promotes an understanding and appreciation of the diverse cultural traditions in U.S. society.

The authors conclude:

The insidious effect of taken-for-granted assumptions is the way they interconnect with and reify one another in a seemingly logical set of relationships . . . . If, on the other hand, educators begin with a belief in the transformative role of education, the value of accessing diversity, a faith in the potential success of every student, a commitment to collaborative and political linkages with parents and communities, then mustering the inventiveness to create new ways of organizing on behalf of children would be the logical, moral, and just thing to do (Astuto et al., p. 41).

The purpose of the following chapters is twofold. First, we wish to provide a comprehensive, research-based synthesis of the dynamics contributing to the academic achievement patterns of urban students. Second, these chapters offer research and theory to inform decision making and influence urban school reform strategies being developed by:
- legislators responsible for policies and resource allocations,
- teacher preparation institutions,
- educators,
- community leaders and parents, and
- educational researchers.

In Chapter 2, Wang and Kovach highlight historical and present-day social dynamics that contribute to conditions in urban communities, districts, and schools. The authors place schools at the center of a host of interconnected social problems that include urban poverty, crime, and inadequate health care; discuss the influences of family and community on learning that occurs outside of school; and describe the conditions for learning in schools. They propose a two-part initiative to foster resilience: (1) school-linked, comprehensive, coordinated child and family services; and (2) elementary and secondary school experiences that are inclusive, integrated, appropriate, and meaningful.

The next chapter, by Greenfield, Raeff, and Quiroz, provides an overview of human development in the urban context. The authors explore current theory and research on restructuring urban education and describe the broader cultural value systems that shape minority and immigrant children in the United States. They also discuss differences in the experiences and cultural value systems of minority students and compare them to the cultural value systems of public schools, formulating an explanation of the "invisible cultures" of students and schools.

The next three chapters, contributed by Zeichner, Stevens, and Benard, outline what needs to be done in urban schools and classrooms to improve teaching and learning. Zeichner identifies issues of pedagogy and contextualizes teaching and learning to describe what teachers in urban classrooms need to be like, to know, and to be able to do to teach all students. He defines cultural congruence in instruction, recommends a focus on "meaning making," describes reciprocal teaching, and emphasizes the importance of teachers believing in their own ability to teach urban students and in their students' ability to learn.

Opportunity to learn (OTL) includes more than a narrow focus on conditions external to teaching and learning that contribute to underachievement. Stevens, in Chapter 5, "calls attention to not only standards for instructional quality, but also for school and family support structures." Opportunity to learn variables focus on what teachers do and address issues of equity and accountability. Stevens categorizes these variables as content coverage, content exposure, content emphasis, and quality of instructional delivery. She adds to this mix three variables that are closely related to students' academic achievement: family support, school environment and climate, and students' performance and behavior. Stevens describes how opportunity to learn changes the perception and interpretation of student outcome data, along with approaches for measuring OTL variables.

Benard (Chapter 6) charges that the scapegoating of kids, their families, and schools by others in society negatively impacts the men, women, and children—usually of color—who inhabit our poverty-stricken inner cities. According to this author, labeling poor urban children "at-risk" and viewing the results of poverty as a personal deficiency or family or cultural deprivation fails to name the full face of poverty and reinforces public indifference. The growing body of international, cross-cultural, developmental research supports a change in our thinking about students who are at-risk to students who are resilient. A focus on social competence, problem-solving skills, autonomy, and a sense of purpose and future supports the development of protective coping strategies. Benard discusses three ways schools can encourage resilience in students: by providing caring and support, by holding high expectations, and by giving students opportunities for meaningful participation in their education.

In Chapter 7, Louis and Smith delineate the requirements for changing and supporting classroom practice. They describe the improvement of teacher engagement as a necessary and central target of urban school reform. "Unless teachers engage in teaching and feel that they are effective, students are less likely to make rapid progress in learning. . . . This is particularly true for schools with a high concentration of lower income and minority students," maintain Louis and Smith with support from research. Improvement requires organizational structures that provide a clear mission, respect and caring for students, emphasis on staff closeness, support, and a demand for active problem solving among teachers.

All of these authors introduce challenging ideas and outline the necessary strategies for addressing the dynamics that shape urban communities, schools, and students.

REFERENCES

Astuto, T., D.L. Clark, A. Read, K. McGree, and L.P. Fernandez. (1993). *Challenges to Dominant Assumptions Controlling Educational Reform.* Andover, Mass.: The Regional Laboratory for Educational Improvement of the Northeast and Islands.

Bartelt, D.W. (1994). "The Macroecology of Educational Outcomes." In *School/Community Connections: Exploring Issues for Research and Practice,* edited by L.C. Rigsby, M.C. Reynolds, and M.C. Wang. San Francisco, Calif.: Jossey-Bass.

Bluestone, B., and B. Harrison. (1982). *The Deindustrialization of America.* New York: Basic Books.

Brown, F. (1994). "Brown and the Politics of Equality." *The Urban Review* 26, 4: 227-242.

Commission on Chapter 1. (1992). *Making Schools Work for Children in Poverty.* Washington, D.C.: American Association for Higher Education.

Council of the Great City Schools. (1994). *National Urban Education Goals: 1992-93 Indicators Report.* Washington, D.C.: Author.

Haberman, M. (1991). "The Pedagogy of Poverty Versus Good Teaching." *Phi Delta Kappan* 73, 4: 290-294.

Hodgekinson, H.L. (1985). *All One System: Demographics of Education—Kindergarten Through Graduate School.* Washington, D.C.: Institute for Educational Leadership.

Kozol, J. (1991). *Savage Inequalities: Children in America's Schools.* New York: Crown.

Lytle, J.H. (1992). "Prospects for Reforming Urban Schools." *Urban Education* 27, 2: 109-131.

Maguin, E. (September 1994). "Academic Performance and Its Relationship to Delinquency." Paper presented at the Summit Conference on Learning Disabilities, Washington, D.C.

Newmann, F.M. (1993). "Beyond Common Sense in Educational Restructuring: The Issues of Content and Linkage." *Educational Researcher* 22, 2: 4-22.

O'Connor, J. (1973). *The Fiscal Crisis of the State.* New York: St. Martin's Press.

O'Day, J.A., and M.S. Smith. (1993). "Systemic Reform and Educational Opportunity." In *Designing Coherent Education Policy: Improving the System,* edited by S.H. Fuhrman. San Francisco, Calif.: Jossey-Bass.

Orfield, G. (1994). *The Growth of Segregation in American Schools: Changing Patterns of Segregation and Poverty Since 1968.* Alexandria, Va.: National School Boards Association.

Ottinger, C., and M. Root. (1994). *Critical Educational Trends: A Poll of America's Urban Schools.* Washington, D.C.: Council of the Great City Schools.

Passow, A.H. (1992). "Urban Schools a Second (?) or Third (?) Time Around: Priorities for Curricular and Instructional Reform." *Education and Urban Society* 23, 3: 243-255.

Urban Education Project. (1994). *The Urban Learner Framework: An Overview.* Philadelphia, Pa.: Research for Better Schools.

Williams, B., and E. Newcombe. (1994). "Building on the Strengths of Urban Learners." *Educational Leadership* 51, 8: 75-78.

Yancey, W.L., and S.J. Saporito. (1994). "Ecological Embeddedness of Educational Processes and Outcomes." In *School/Community Connections: Exploring Issues for Research and Practice,* edited by L.C. Rigsby, M.C. Reynolds, and M.C. Wang. San Francisco, Calif.: Jossey-Bass.

2

Bridging the Achievement Gap in Urban Schools: Reducing Educational Segregation and Advancing Resilience-Promoting Strategies

MARGARET C. WANG AND JOHN A. KOVACH

The Supreme Court's 1954 decision in *Brown v. Board of Education of Topeka, Kansas*, made equal access to public education the law of the land. With each decade we have increased the proportion of the U.S. population in school, included children from more diverse sociocultural and economic backgrounds, and diversified the kinds of educational programs offered. Indeed, by emphasizing the value of education and its potential as a tool for social and economic equality, we have made enormous progress in ensuring equal access to a free public education for all children and youth in the United States.

But these accomplishments have fallen far short of the vision of a universal school system that provides all children with equal access to success in school. Much of the school desegregation activity of the past three decades has been motivated by a desire to end segregation of students from ethnic and language minority backgrounds. To date, these efforts have produced very little change to enhance social and academic integration (Bartelt 1994a, Yancey and Saporito 1995). Furthermore, the focus on the "setting" of schooling has become a major barrier to the nation's quest to improve school for the very students who are the intended beneficiaries of desegregation (Lipsky and Gartner 1989, Wang and Reynolds 1995).

There is little argument about the need to improve our capacity to provide for healthy development and educational success for all U.S. children and youth, including and particularly minority students from economically disadvantaged backgrounds who live in some of the most adverse inner-city situations. School has been and should continue to be the primary focus in finding ways to improve our capacity to provide healthy development and educational success for all children and youth. Other efforts surely will come to naught if we fail to offer powerful forms of education in schools. However, significant learning occurs outside schools, and the conditions for learning in schools are greatly influenced by the family and all elements of the community.

We can cull much information about overcoming adversities from research and practical applications of innovative practices (Wang and Gordon 1994). Despite the difficulties of urban life, cities contain many rich and promising resources for children and families. If only we can find the means of magnifying the "positives" in urban life, we can rekindle hope for improving our capacity for education in urban communities. The purpose of this chapter is twofold:

• to examine the impact of the changing macroecological characteristics of cities on school performance, and

• to glean from the research base and innovative developments what we can do to make a significant difference in reducing the achievement gap among urban students from ethnic and language minority backgrounds.

INNER CITIES IN DECLINE:
A MACROECOLOGICAL PERSPECTIVE

There is increasing recognition that the achievement gap in U.S. urban schools may be better understood in terms of the decentralization of cities, the resulting changes in the social ecology of neighborhoods, and the structure of the urban labor market (Massey and Denton 1993). The contention is that the changing makeup of cities accounts for much of the failure of urban schools. The socioeconomic contexts of schooling—such as differences in ethnicity, socioeconomic class, family and community resources (both social and economic), and patterns of residential and educational segregation—play important roles in differences in educational attainment (Bartelt 1994a, Kantor and Brenzel 1993).

Census data from the 1990s show that the United States leads the industrialized world in numbers of children living in poverty. This is reflected in such legislation as the *Goals 2000: Educate America Act*, the *School-to-Work Opportunities Act*, and the reauthorization of the *Elementary and Secondary Education Act*. Accompanying the decline of the manufacturing base of the U.S. economy and the economic restructuring of cities, there has been an unprecedented increase in the numbers of children and families living in segregated and often highly adverse circumstances that place those children at risk of school failure (Bartelt 1994a, Children's Defense Fund 1992, National Commission on Children 1991).

There is an increasing national recognition of the plight of children and families in a variety of high-risk circumstances and of their need for interventions that foster educational resilience and learning success. Paradoxically, the problem of residential segregation by race and social class actually has grown worse despite efforts following civil rights legislation of the late 1960s (Massey and Denton 1993). The current conditions largely can be traced to two separate but related processes.

First, and most noticeably, the city of the late 20th century is decentralized. Whatever one calls this modern phenomenon—sprawl, edge city, megalopolis, or the malling of the United States—the Dickensian world of the 19th century, with its crowded, narrow streets, and bustling city tenements is largely a thing of the past.

Second, the nature of the economic activity that undergirds urban life has changed dramatically. The urban explosion of the late 19th and early 20th century was fueled by factories and railroads and by immigrants looking for work. Mass education in that era taught work discipline, common language, and rudimentary mathematical skills (Katz 1971). In the late 20th century, the U.S. economy has changed to a service sector economy (Noyelle and Stanbeck 1984) and expectations have grown regarding the nature of job skills within, at least, upper-level service occupations (e.g., medical, legal, management).

The movement of resources, jobs, and people from central city to suburb has created a hostile environment for children, families, and institutions embedded in the cities, including schools. In an analysis of the relationship between microsocial forces and educational accomplishment in the macroecology of 53 major cities across the country, Bartelt (1994b) noted that "inner-city schools are increasingly the schools of remnant populations and communities trapped by their economic irrelevance or their links to diminished labor markets. [They] are increasingly dependent on an overloaded and endangered fiscal base" (p. 2).

The increase in residential segregation and thereby educational segregation in urban schools is as much an economic as a social response to the decentralization of cities and the changing urban economic order. These changes, taken together, translate into a marked achievement gap between urban schools and the national norms. Indeed, the mean reading score of a school's students can be predicted by the aggregated rates of childhood poverty and the various epidemiological problems. The more a school draws from poor neighborhoods riddled with social problems, the worse its students perform academically. Yancey and Saporito (1994) found that children from inner-city neighborhoods are more likely to contract everything from measles to tuberculosis to lead poisoning. As poverty rises, both children and young adults are more likely to be crime victims, to receive inadequate health care, and to suffer from a variety of physical, psychological, and social traumas. These circumstances place children at risk of educational failure and, by necessity, place schools at the center of interconnected social problems.

THE CONTEMPORARY CONTEXT OF EDUCATIONAL SEGREGATION

Despite legislative mandates and progress in achieving school integration that transcends neighborhood boundaries, educational segregation—or "resegregation" within integrated schools—is rampant and maintains a status quo that continues to contribute to the achievement gap (Wang 1986). The situation has not improved since the publication of Coleman's (1966) findings on the lack of progress with desegregation in the decade following the *Brown* decision. Schools are still largely segregated today. In 1968, for example, 76 percent of African American students and 55 percent of Latino students attended predominately minority schools. In 1991, these statistics had improved only slightly for African Americans and had grown worse for Latinos—66 percent of all African Americans and 74.3 percent of Latinos were still in segregated schools (Celis 1993). In states such as Illinois, Michigan, New York, and New Jersey, more than 50 percent of the schools are 90 to 100 percent minority.

The negative impact of residential segregation—both on the composition of the school population and the quality of education—continues to raise pressing concerns in the educational community and the public. A primary problem associated with residential segregation is the prevalence of the achievement gap. African American and other minority students tend to be in schools where overall achievement is low (Bartelt 1994a). In a January 1995 opinion (*Pennsylvania Human Relations Commission v. School District of Philadelphia*), Judge Doris Smith decreed that the School District of Philadelphia must "end the School District's 24 years of stonewalling and claims of fiscal inability to educate the racially isolated school students, and to . . . finally satisfy its legal obligation to those children" (p. 12). She argued that measures can be enacted in segregated systems that will move the schools toward educational equity, including eliminating prolonged disruption in learning at the beginning of each school year; providing textbooks and other necessary supplies at each school; assigning qualified substitutes in racially isolated schools; and developing incentives to attract more experienced teachers to those schools. In essence, the decree does not require increased integration of schools but does command equity in educational outcomes.

Efforts directed toward achieving racial integration in schools, although well intentioned, have created even greater segregation for a large number of students in urban schools. According to Yancey and Saporito (1994), magnet school and choice busing strategies have actually resulted in greater homogeneity in racial and socioeconomic makeup in neighborhood schools. Moreover, even in schools that have achieved racial integration, students from ethnic and language minority backgrounds often are resegregated by a variety of pullout remedial or compensatory education programs (Heller, Holtzman, and Messick 1982). These categorical programs, generally created to serve students with identified problems, are governed by separate funding streams and eligibility criteria; their implementation often results in added layers of bureaucracy and disjointed implementation, with further segregation for large numbers of children from ethnic and language minority backgrounds (Heller et al. 1982, Lipsky and Gartner 1989, National Association of State Boards of Education Study Group on Special Education 1992).

The school reassignment approach to school desegregation often obscures the multiple ways by which children can be segregated socially and academically in school. Minority students frequently are reassigned to integrated schools but then resegregated by their placement in "special" programs. Here we refer to a somewhat different form of segregation—educational segregation via so-called second system programs initiated to respond to the diversity of student needs, such as Chapter 1, Title I, and special education programs. A special commission appointed to investigate the problem of overrepresentation of minority students in special education found that African American students are two to three times more likely than whites to be labeled retarded or behaviorally disturbed (Heller et al. 1982).

Once assigned to pullout programs, children's learning problems may actually increase. Substantial evidence shows that students receive inferior instruction when they are assigned to specially designed programs, thereby placing them further at risk of educational failure. In many cases, selecting and tracking students for instruction in special programs are based on certain perceived student differences, involving delivery of radically different and not always appropriate content (Allington and Johnston 1989, Oakes 1985). In general, there is a tendency to underestimate what students placed in special programs can do, to neglect fundamental content, to provide less instruction focusing on higher-order thinking and advanced skills, to delay the introduction of more challenging work, and to fail to provide students with a motivating context for learning (Means and Knapp 1991).

A CIVIL RIGHTS ISSUE OF THE 1990S

To counter trends and reduce the achievement gap requires both an inclusive approach to student diversity and powerful instruction that will lead to educational success for all students (National Commission on Chapter 1 1992; Pugach 1995; and Renzulli, Reis, Hebert, and Diaz 1995). The overall problem of school integration should remain on the agenda, but providing quality education must be the central civil rights issue of today. If real progress is to be realized in achieving school success for all children and youth, educational improvement efforts must address whether equal opportunity for education leads to equity in educational outcomes. Providing "opportunities" for education without being accountable for educational outcomes simply perpetuates in a more subtle form the injustices that the *Brown* decision attempted to rectify.

Undoing these injustices will require a major redefinition of educational equity. The way we think about differences among students, how we view the purposes of elementary and secondary education, the way we choose to organize schools, and the forging of school connections with families and communities are all fundamental to the principle that standards of educational outcomes must be upheld for every student. The challenge is in identifying practices that deny, and those that promote, the right to schooling success.

Nowhere are the problems and needs of children as great as in inner cities. Inner cities are like backwater regions, left behind and isolated from an emerging global economy. The widespread problem of academic failure in urban schools, which could cripple the next generation, is sometimes overshadowed by the litany of troubles that plague the urban landscape. But this view of the urban United States is just half of the picture. Cities also contain many rich and promising resources for children and families. Despite the difficulties of life, many children and youth do (and can be nurtured to) mature into healthy adults. One thing is certain: Human development and education must be key considerations in the rebuilding process.

Much is known from the research and practical application of innovative practices that can be used in overcoming adversities and strengthening the resources and protective mechanisms to foster healthy development and educational resilience of children and youth in a variety of situations that place them at risk of school failure (Wang and Gordon 1994, Wang and Reynolds 1995). Children who grow into competent, well-educated adults have a chance to rise above the problems of adverse life circumstances. If only we can find the means to magnify the "positives" in the lives of urban children and youth, we can rekindle hope for progress in addressing the deep-rooted problem of the achievement gap.

Schools are part of a larger system; they are ecologically embedded institutions that confront on a daily basis the problems of their surrounding communities, as well as those of national and multinational institutions—even though the school itself is localized in its point of delivery. It is not possible to achieve significant school improvement without forging working connections with multiple forces that influence the development of children or the social ecology of neighborhoods. The capability of the schools can be greatly enhanced when insights and expertise are drawn from many disciplines and professions and when family and community resources are harnessed to forge a coordinated approach to fostering resilience development and learning success.

FOSTERING EDUCATIONAL RESILIENCE

Resilience, which originated as a construct in developmental psychopathology (Garmezy 1974), has received much attention as an integrative framework for identifying and understanding individual and institutional resources that can be cultivated and mobilized to moderate the effects of individual vulnerability or environmental hazards. Perhaps more than any group, children and youth in urban schools shoulder the burden of the numerous modern morbidities that continue to plague urban life, including enormous demographic and economic transformations; the resulting upswing of poverty, unemployment, and residential and educational segregation; the disjointed pattern of service delivery; and ineffective schools.

Broadly conceived in the context of achieving learning success, resilience is a construct that not only can be applied to individual and family situations but also within institutions, such as communities and the schools that serve them (Wang and Gordon 1994). Resilience development, when applied in the context of schooling, is understood in terms of the complex interrelationships that characterize the development and functioning of the resilient individual and the protective mechanisms (family, school, and community) that foster such patterns of resilience. Much discussion among educators has centered on the search for resilience-promoting strategies or protective mechanisms that magnify the circumstances within which the burden of adversity is reduced and opportunities for learning are advanced. Two major guidelines, emerging from the past three decades of research and innovative development efforts, have received increasing recognition for potentially reducing the risk factors associated with urban life and the achievement gap in urban schools:

• Forging greater school connections with families and the community to support resilience development and student learning.

• Reducing educational segregation within schools and implementing responsive and powerful instructional practices to ensure learning success of every student.

FORGING SCHOOL CONNECTIONS WITH FAMILIES AND COMMUNITIES

The educational reforms of the 1990s have been marked by the urgency of addressing the increasingly dire circumstances surrounding this nation's children. Families, particularly those from ethnic and language minority backgrounds who live in poverty, are beset by life-threatening problems that place their children at risk of educational failure. Public and private community agencies provide services such as counseling, financial assistance, or medical treatment to overcome concurrent problems or risks, but service delivery is often carried out in an isolated fashion. Schools are part of this disconnected nonsystem (Council of Chief State School Officers 1989, Levy and Copple 1989, Schorr and Schorr 1988). There is a growing public demand for a coordinated and inclusive approach to service delivery (Center for the Future of Children and the David and Lucile Packard Foundation 1992; Tyack 1992; Wang, Haertel, and Walberg 1995).

Students facing many adversities benefit from increased access to the range of services provided in collaborative arrangements. There is increasing recognition that the learning problems of children and families cannot be tackled by schools alone and that broader social policies must be established to initiate interagency, collaborative programs that link schools and other service agencies. How educators and staff in various organizations can enhance one another's efforts to ensure physical and psychological well-being and learning success of children and youth has become the central systemic school reform agenda of the 1990s (Kirst and Kelley 1995, Wang and Reynolds 1995). This focus is clearly reflected in special reports (e.g., National Commission on Chapter 1 1992, Committee for Economic Development 1994); in recently enacted legislation (e.g., *Goals 2000: Educate America Act* and the *Improving America's Schools Act*); and in the research base from varied disciplines (Rigsby, Reynolds, and Wang 1995).

A variety of innovative strategies and programs that are effective in forging coordinated, comprehensive delivery of education and related human services are being created across the country (Center for the Future of Children and the David and Lucile Packard Foundation 1992; Council of Chief State School Officers 1989; Wang, Haertel, and Walberg 1994, 1995; U.S. Department of Education 1995). Although they vary in their approaches and in the specifics of program design, these strategies share several common premises. One is that the problems facing children and families stem from a variety of cultural, economic, political, and health problems. Their solutions are by nature complex, and they require pooling of resources from public and private sector agencies such as city and state health and human services departments, businesses, religious institutions, and community-based social and medical service agencies. They also require negotiation of new forms of cooperation and coordination and new ways of mobilizing the energies and resources of the community.

A second premise is that narrowly conceived plans and commitments that focus only on schools will not solve the growing problems that must be addressed to ensure success of the many children and youth who have not fared well under the current system of service delivery. The challenge is to understand thoroughly the problems and resources that can be drawn upon to help raise consciousness about the opportunities in the community, especially among those who are in a position to shape policies, and to provide resources to improve the prospects of learning success for children and youth in at-risk situations.

A third premise is that school-linked, coordinated, comprehensive services for children and families can meet the diverse needs of students especially well. Collaboratives often address multiple problems of families who are frequently in communities that are educationally, economically, and socially marginalized. They are poised to provide learning environments that support learning success through focusing on the physical and social wellness needs of students, providing role models and new information skills, and linking with the many resilience-enhancing resources of the community.

The following is a sample list of effective features of school-linked, comprehensive, coordinated child and family services, drawn from findings of a comprehensive review of the research base (Wang et al. 1994, 1995):

• The needs of students in at-risk circumstances are best addressed by collaborative programs that are prevention oriented, serve multiple needs, and target the family for intervention.

• The use of case management preserves an orientation toward serving the needs of the whole child and reduces fragmentation of service delivery.

• An ample planning period during which the perspectives of all stakeholders can be taken into account is essential to the healthy development of the collaborative. During this planning time, written agreements describing new roles, responsibilities, and procedures can be developed to guide the collaborative's operation. The use of needs assessment can be a helpful planning tool.

• Resolving issues of child and family confidentiality facilitates information sharing by collaborative staff.

• The provision of adequate resources (money, time, space, professional expertise, enthusiasm) is essential to program operation.

• Establishing shared decision-making and management procedures contributes to a sense of equal partnership among school and agency personnel. Concerns such as common eligibility criteria and common outcomes for evaluative purposes must be addressed.

• Well-crafted technical assistance should be provided to collaborative staff. Potential topics include increased communication and collegiality; goals clarification; cultural, ethnic, and linguistic sensitivity; client confidentiality; sharing information that can enhance teachers' instruction and classroom management; and new roles and responsibilities for participating in the collaborative.

• The location of services is a central issue in the collaborative's effectiveness. Locating services together reduces fragmentation of service delivery and enhances the likelihood that clients will receive the array of services needed. Collaborative programs that provide services together can respond efficiently to the needs of children and families beset by multiple academic, medical, and mental health problems.

• The evolving role of school personnel in collaborative school-linked services challenges existing school structures. Teachers' involvement in referrals and case management procedures needs to be defined. Feedback from service providers to teachers could be used to tailor instruction and classroom management to meet the needs of troubled students. The roles of teachers and school personnel in collaboratives could be further expanded to better meet the demands of students and families in at-risk circumstances.

• Serving families, including the needs of individual parents, is believed to be essential to the success of collaborative, school-linked services. A range of medical, mental health, legal, and social services are being provided to students and families. Rarely are basic needs—such as food, shelter, and transportation, as well as emergency services—made available.

• Financing a collaborative requires access to stable funding that is not susceptible to the vagaries of year-to-year state budgets or limited research monies. Collaboratives need to access current funding set aside for children and family services.

• A variety of outcome measures should be used to evaluate collaborative school-linked services. Outcome measures should represent the goals of all participating agencies, not just schools. Family-based outcomes should be collected. Student achievement scores, attendance data, and dropout rates can be used for comparisons in multisite program evaluations, but additional outcomes should be collected. Direct measures of collaboration, numbers and kinds of services provided, unobtrusive measures, and client satisfaction can provide additional information on the collaborative's success.

Following are selected examples of effective collaborative programs.

The Children's Aid Society's Community Schools Program. The overall goal of the program is to extend the use of existing facilities so they become multiservice centers providing all services required by neighborhood children and families. The services provided through the program include: health services, before- and after-school programs, academic support, career readiness, arts and recreation programs, parent resources, summer programs, and community development.

Findings on program outcomes show increases in both math and reading achievement, and data indicate that the program has bolstered attendance to the highest in the district. Furthermore, there were no reports of violence, property destruction, or graffiti. These latter findings are particularly significant because the program was implemented in areas where school violence typically is an everyday occurrence.

Stetson Middle School's Learning City Program. Stetson Middle School is located in an inner-city community in Philadelphia. It is an area surrounded by drug gang territory with abandoned factories and rundown houses. The overall goal of the Learning City Program is the radical improvement of student learning through linking schools with all other learning environments, including the home, library, museums, the workplace, colleges and universities, and other public and private sector establishments.

The Learning City Program was designed as a delivery framework to forge a coordinated approach to educational and related services delivery to provide more effective school response to student diversity and to ensure student learning success. Key design features of the Learning City Program include:

• A site-specific implementation plan that takes into account the school's improvement needs, the learning characteristics of students, staff expertise and staffing patterns, the curriculums, and other implementation resources.

• A schoolwide organizational support system and learning process that involves regular and specialist teachers in the planning and delivery of instruction in regular classroom settings.

• A data-based staff development program. Training for school personnel begins before program implementation and continues through the school year, on the basis of staff needs.

• An instructional learning management system that focuses on the development of student self-responsibility for behavior and learning progress.

• An integrated diagnostic-prescriptive process that provides a learning plan individually designed for each student. The process includes the use of whole-class and small-group instruction, as well as one-on-one tutoring, based on an ongoing analysis of student needs, resource availability, and instructional expediency.

• An adaptive approach to family and community involvement. The Learning City Program encourages an active program of family involvement to increase communication and cooperation between home and school and to facilitate establishment of a shared partnership approach to improving educational outcomes of every student.

• A school-linked human and health services component that fosters community partnerships to support individual student learning.

In addition to Stetson Middle School in Philadelphia, several schools across the country use the Learning City Program as the basic framework for reform. School implementation of the Learning City Program is coordinated with governmental agencies such as health and human services, housing, and law enforcement to ensure that the social and physical needs of the students and families are addressed in timely and responsive ways. In essence, the program aims to raise the expectation that providing quality learning experiences for children and families is at the core of community revitalization efforts.

To date, findings among schools implementing the Learning City Program show a general pattern of more positive perceptions about learning compared to students in comparison schools (Wang, Oates, and Weishen 1995). Students in schools with the Learning City Program tend to perceive better and more constructive feedback from teachers about their work and behaviors, a higher level of aspiration for academic learning, and better academic self-concept. The data also show a positive pattern of changes in math and reading scores and that students tend to score higher than their counterparts in comparison schools not implementing the program.

Other noteworthy findings include increased participation of families and the community in a wide range of school activities and in the decision-making process about school programs. As a result of their involvement in one school, for example, a school-based health clinic was put in place by the community and the local children's hospital. And, as part of a health initiative in another Learning City school, the school planning team arranged for monthly visits from a local hospital, bringing medical teams to provide immunization, check-ups, and follow-up care to children and families.

Texas School of the Future Project. This project was designed to improve the lives of the many Texas children in need and, at the same time, circumvent the problems created by so many existing programs that are diverse, single focused, and uncoordinated. The program is being implemented in four major Texas cities: San Antonio, Houston, Dallas, and Austin.

The program consists of health services, mental health services, recreational and family support, parent education, parental involvement, conflict resolution, and gang prevention. Data collected to examine the program's efficacy include: self-esteem, school climate, academic achievement, and mental and physical health. Although implementation at the four sites differs in emphasis and strategies, data from initial implementation showed notable differences in student self-report of mental and physical health among students participating in the program when compared with those not in the program.

The San Antonio School of the Future Project is designed with family support as a centerpiece. The project is located in J.T. Brackenridge Elementary School, where the majority of students are from one of the oldest federal housing projects in the nation (officially housing 1,000 families). The school is adjacent to the housing project. More than 54 percent of the children in the community reside in single-parent homes. Unemployment is high. Family violence and substance abuse are frequent.

The initial two years of program implementation consisted of the following: family, individual, and group therapy; advocacy and education concerning social services; parent education and development of a parent volunteer core; programs that provide alternatives to violence; use of outside volunteers to provide expanded support services; increased participation of parents and students in school management; and expanded involvement of private corporations in the program.

The Houston School of the Future Project encompasses three schools, the Hogg Middle School and two elementary schools that feed into it. Implementation in Houston aims to achieve three specific objectives: to increase and improve the quality of parental involvement at each school; to obtain needed resources for children; and to coordinate resources so that service delivery occurs in a smooth and natural manner. A key feature of the Houston project is the Partnership Council, through which the project receives systematic input from the direct service provider. The Council helps ensure that the lines of communication among the various service agencies stay open. The Partnership Council includes representatives from private sector institutions such as an accounting firm, a law firm, IBM, and Apple Computers; county court services; and civic and educational agencies such as Leadership 2000 and the University of Texas Health Science Center.

The Dallas School of the Future Project was designed as a model for dynamic change. It consists of three schools (two elementary and one middle) situated in the southern sector of the city, with primarily African American and secondarily Latino students. The two elementary schools are located in a large education complex that used to be a shopping center. The physical setting, in conjunction with modern renovations, provides a roomy, colorful, and well-equipped primary school environment that includes community meeting rooms, a Head Start site, and space for a wellness center and community service agencies or satellite agencies participating in the project. The Dallas Project mainly consists of five program components: core innovations, such as the site-based team of parents and educators and the mental health team; coordination of community services; innovations in school programs; bringing existing school programs and services into the school site; and health and wellness programs.

The Austin Model for School of the Future focuses on creating a sense of community. The project consists of one elementary and one middle school. The Austin Project, as with the other School of the Future Projects, has worked closely with the existing connections that the Hogg Foundation has built with the community and schools. The initial activities include a program of recreation activities that are sponsored by the Austin Police Department, parent support programs, teacher support programs, community awareness efforts, and partnering with existing efforts.

REDUCING EDUCATIONAL SEGREGATION WITHIN SCHOOLS

Inclusion or integration of children with special needs in regular school environments has received increasing support as a systemic educational improvement strategy (National Commission on Chapter 1 1992, McDonnell and Hill 1993, National Association of State Boards of Education Study Group on Special Education 1992, Reynolds 1989, U.S. Department of Education 1994, Will 1986). As schools are challenged to effectively serve an increasingly diverse student population, the central improvement question is not whether to provide an inclusive system of education and related service delivery but *how to implement* such a system in ways that are feasible and effective in ensuring schooling success for all children, including and especially those with special needs.

Efforts to integrate children with special needs in regular classrooms have been shown to positively affect both academic learning and social relations with classmates (Allington 1987; Baker, Wang, and Walberg 1994; Carlsburg and Kavale 1980; Jenkins, Pious, and Peterson 1988; Wang and Reynolds 1995). Contrary to the conventional belief, findings from a recently completed meta-analysis of studies published between 1983 and 1992 on the effects of inclusion on learning indicate that segregation of students with special needs in separate classrooms is actually deleterious to their academic performance and social adjustment, and special students perform better on average in regular classrooms (Baker et al. 1994). These findings have bolstered the increasing demands by parents and legal experts for schools to address the scientific and legal basis for noninclusive practices (*Oberti v. Clementon 1993, Pennsylvania Human Relations Commis-*

sion v. School District of Pennsylvania 1973, 1994) and to explain why so many students are set aside in categorical programs in which they continue to fall behind their peers. Indeed, many students require much better help then they now receive. They often have unusual needs (both at the high and low margins of the achievement distribution) and challenge teachers to the limits of their commitment, insight, and skills.

Clearly we must find ways to reform current practices to ensure that the educational experience in elementary and secondary schools is appropriate, meaningful, and the main source for positive development and education for all students. There is a substantial knowledge base that should be used to improve the current disjointed and unresponsive approach to caring for the many children and youth who are not adequately served by the current system. The following highlights are drawn from recommendations that evolved through discussions at a national invitational conference on "Making a Difference for Students at Risk" (Wang and Reynolds 1994). A transcending principle that emerged from the recommendations is that public schools should be inclusive and integrated, and separation by race, gender, language background, ability, or any other characteristic should be minimal and should require a compelling rationale.

• **Make public schools inclusive and integrated.** A "sunset" date is suggested for all legislation affecting categorical programs, as is a date for organizing efforts to develop coherent, broadly framed revisions of federal policies and programs in all domains. It is suggested that these programs should: (1) reduce all forms of "set-asides" or segregation of students; (2) decrease suspensions, expulsions, and dropouts; and (3) place burden-of-proof obligations on those who propose separating a student from the mainstream program.

• **Organize public schools into smaller units—minischools, charters, or houses—in which groups of students remain together for several years of study.** This would allow increased use of site-based management; curricular options and choice by students, teachers, and parents; and heterogenous and cross-age grouping. It also would facilitate the design and implementation of major curriculum and instruction innovations.

• **Step up research on the learning characteristics and needs of students, with particular attention to students with special needs,**

to provide a growing knowledge base and credible evaluation system. Research should address strengths, resilience, and other positive factors as well as limitations and deficiencies for all children. A case can be made for disaggregating research data for subgroups such as race and gender. This does not imply physical separation of students within the school; it does, however, show how various racial, ethnic, and gender groups are advancing in their learning under various conditions.

• **Implement new approaches based on what is known about teaching in schools with a high concentration of students with special needs.** Here the emphasis is on aggressive teaching, with high learning expectations for all students.

• **Shift the use of labels from students to programs.** Children will be better served if educators use diagnostic procedures emphasizing variables that can be manipulated to improve learning. As an initial step, educators should identify students who need extra help. Most students who are served by the various categorical programs that label them need some individualized education rather than a different kind of education.

• **Expand programs for the most able students.** Programs to nurture the potentials of the most able students are one of the most neglected areas in urban schools. To make advances in learning, these students require expert instruction, which is typically only present in areas such as athletics and music. Equally important is to make strenuous efforts to give students from disadvantaged backgrounds opportunities to show their potential for accelerated learning. Once they do, challenging programs should be made available to them with continuing support.

• **Apply concepts of inclusion and integration to the bureaucratic structure of government, professional organizations, and advocacy groups.** If educational programs are to become more coherent and integrated, the public and professional structures that uphold them must pull together. Federal and state agencies need to become integrated, and funding across all categorical programs, as well as monitoring systems, must be revised to emphasize teamwork and coordination.

• **Integrate the most current findings in general, remedial, and special education, as well as special language learning areas, into** professional development programs of all educational profession-als. For inclusive forms of education to work, regular teachers and specialist professionals must be equipped with expertise to take on new or altered roles. Newly emerging practices that aim to more ef-fectively respond to student diversity, such as minischools, must be incorporated in continuing professional development of the school staff.

• **Create broad cross-agency collaboration for delivering coordi-nated, comprehensive child and family services.** Various levels and divisions of government agencies often undertake separate, uncoordi-nated programs aimed to support healthy development and learning of children and families in a variety of disadvantaged circumstances. Implementation of community rebuilding efforts, such as the Empow-erment Zones or Enterprise Communities, for example, are rarely linked with "education empowering" efforts. Education must be a key connection to enable children and families to take stock of the benefits of a broad-based community rebuilding effort.

Inclusive and instructionally powerful learning environments can be used as a strategy for reducing the achievement gap. Here are some successful examples:

Johnson City Mastery Learning Model for Achieving Student Suc-cess. This program is an outcome-driven developmental model based on the philosophy that all students can achieve subject mastery and other desired outcomes if given sufficient time and the proper learn-ing conditions. It entails a comprehensive, systematic change process that is applied to all aspects of school operation: instruction, curricu-lum design, climate, leadership and management, staff development, and flow of communication.

The delivery system of the Johnson City Model involves exten-sive curriculum planning and ongoing curriculum revision, tailored to meet the needs of the students. Curriculum development is staff di-rected and research based. Teams of teachers, coordinators, and prin-cipals develop objectives by unit and discipline. Staff are assigned based on student needs. A strong emphasis is placed on communica-tion at all levels—administration, teachers, parents, and students.

In addition to achieving a thorough understanding and mastery of their subjects, students are expected to become self-directed learners and to exhibit concern for others and for the environment. Substantial data indicate significant improvements in student achievement; morale, climate, and staff effectiveness; and parent and community support of the outcome-driven developmental approach to ensure student mastery and learning success.

The Adaptive Learning Environments Model. Implementing an inclusive approach to student diversity requires a fundamental restructuring of how schools are organized to respond to the individual needs of youth as part of a comprehensive system of delivery of educational and related services in regular school contexts. The Adaptive Learning Environments Model (ALEM), designed as a conceptual framework and a delivery system, has the overall goal of ensuring the learning success of all students, including children with special needs in regular classroom learning environments (Wang 1992). Specific interventions are incorporated as ongoing support to enhance each student's ability to achieve in academic subjects and in developing social competence and self-esteem.

The dual focus of ALEM is an educational approach that effectively responds to student diversity and a process that provides a systematic structure and professional development support for implementation. At the classroom level, the delivery design calls for instructional teaming, heterogenous grouping, flexible scheduling, and continuous progress planning and monitoring. At the school level, the delivery system calls for the use of staffing patterns that promote coordination and collaboration among the school staff. Specialized professions (e.g., special education teachers, Title I teachers, school psychologists, speech pathologists, school social workers) work closely with regular education teachers to plan and serve in a variety of implementation support functions to bolster student learning. They provide critical technical and instructional help by assisting in the diagnostic-prescriptive process, providing direct instruction, and serving as consultants. In addition, ALEM also incorporates a systematic adaptive approach for implementing an active family and community involvement program to forge increased collaboration and communication among the school, the family, and the community.

Findings from close to two decades of research provide constant evidence that a high degree of program implementation can be achieved by schools in a variety of geographic regions with different resource and site-specific constraints and that effective implementation of ALEM leads to positive changes in classroom processes, such as increases in student-teacher interactions for instructional purposes, increases in the time students spend in cooperative learning and peer tutoring, and significant improvements in student achievement.

THE NEXT STEP

Clearly, the present approaches to reducing educational segregation and closing the achievement gap in urban schools are not working acceptably. They do not ensure the kind of accountability intended for achieving equity in educational outcomes of many children and youth from ethnic and language minority backgrounds who live in circumstances that place them at risk of educational failure. If we are to be prepared to face the challenges posed by the demographic, economic, and technological realities, we must begin to make fundamental changes that focus on the rights of all students to schooling success and take into account how to better serve students who are marginalized in schools.

It seems likely that the coming decade will make correcting the faults in present practice a need that is all the more pressing. Greater educational productivity will be necessary to compete in the global economy. Federal and state education agencies and local schools must be linked with other educational, social, and health service institutions to establish priorities in all aspects of urban services to ensure that children and youth receive the highest quality education possible. A common standard of educational outcomes must be upheld for every student, including those in urban schools with high concentrations of students from ethnic and language minority backgrounds. Access to education is one thing; providing quality education that enables all students to succeed in school is quite another.

We must proceed now with the task of breaking through the narrowness, disjointedness, and wastefulness of the categorical approach to providing for student diversity. Programs currently serving large numbers of minority students would profit from rigorous improvement efforts organized around principles of effective practices. We propose a two-part initiative to address the achievement gap in urban schools:

• forge greater school connections with families and the community to foster resilience development, and

• eliminate educational segregation within schools and implement responsive, powerful practices to ensure learning success of every student.

The first part of the initiative we propose involves joining effective practices to establish a coordinated delivery system that better serves the needs of all students and families. The second part calls for broad authority at federal, state, and local levels to grant waivers of rules and regulations to schools that wish to provide more integrated education for all students, including those who are segregated in second-system programs. The conditions of waivers include assurance to parents of accountability in terms of student outcomes and assurance that no financial disincentives are created for schools undertaking such initiatives.

Many worthy ideas and demonstrated practices could be encouraged under our proposed initiatives, including the recommendations suggested in this chapter. The proposed waivers for performance strategy would permit and support the implementation of effective practices to scale, while offering assurances about hard-won rights to parents and students as well as removing financial disincentives for responsible changes.

As we see it, a major next step is an aggressive plan to engage the public in dialogue on the kinds of broad-based school reforms that are needed to significantly reduce educational segregation and the achievement gap. Much is at stake for all of us. It will take much courage to lead the way to new, more coherent, and genuinely useful programs that can make a difference in support of student achievement and to bring the schools into broader collaborative efforts for community betterment. The policy and reform recommendations advanced in this chapter are a call for a better and more systemic approach to delivery of services within and beyond school walls.

REFERENCES

Allington, R.L. (July/August 1987). "Shattered Hopes." *Learning* 87: 60-66.

Allington, R.L., and P. Johnston. (1989). "Coordination, Collaboration, and Consistency: The Redesign of Compensatory and Special Education Intervention." In *Preventing School Failure: Effective Programs for Students At-Risk,* edited by R. Slavin, N. Madden, and N. Karweit. Boston, Mass.: Allyn and Bacon.

Baker, E.T., M.C. Wang, and H.J. Walberg. (1994). "The Effects of Inclusion on Learning." *Educational Leadership* 52, 4: 33-35.

Bartelt, D.W. (1994a). "The Macroecology of Educational Outcomes." In *School-Community Connections: Exploring Issues for Research and Practice,* edited by L.C. Rigsby, M.C. Reynolds, and M.C. Wang. San Francisco, Calif.: Jossey-Bass.

Bartelt, D.W. (1994b). "The Macroecology of Educational Outcomes." *The CEIC Review* 3, 1: 2-3.

Carlsburg, C., and K. Kavale. (1980). "The Efficacy of Special Versus Regular Class Placement for Exceptional Children: A Meta-Analysis." *Journal of Special Education* 14: 295-309.

Celis, A. (December 14, 1993). "Study Finds Rising Concentration of Black and Hispanic Students." *New York Times,* A1.

Center for the Future of Children, and the David and Lucile Packard Foundation. (1992). "School-Linked Services." *The Future of Children* 2, 1: Special focus issue.

Children's Defense Fund. (1992). *The State of America's Children.* Washington, D.C.: Author.

Coleman, J.S. (1966). *Equality of Educational Opportunity.* Washington, D.C.: U.S. Government Printing Office.

Committee for Economic Development. (1994). *Putting Learning First: Governing Schools for High Achievement.* New York: Author.

Council of Chief State School Officers. (1989). *Family Support, Education, and Involvement: A Guide for State Action.* Washington, D.C.: Author.

Garmezy, N. (1974). "Children At Risk: The Search for the Antecedents of Schizophrenia. Part 1. Conceptual Models and Research Methods." *Schizophrenia Bulletin* 8: 14-90.

Heller, K., W. Holtzman, and S. Messick. (1982). *Placing Children in Special Education: A Strategy for Equity.* Washington, D.C.: National Academy of Science Press.

Jenkins, J.R., C. Pious, and D. Peterson. (1988). "Categorical Programs for

Remedial and Handicapped Students: Issues of Validity." *Exceptional Children* 55, 2: 147-158.

Kantor, H., and B. Brenzel. (1993). "Urban Education and the Truly Disadvantaged: The Historical Roots of the Contemporary Crisis, 1945-1990." In *The Underclass Debate: Views from History*, edited by M. Katz. Princeton, N.J.: Princeton University Press.

Katz, M. (1971). *Class, Bureaucracy, and Schools: The Illusion of Educational Change in America*. New York: Praeger.

Kirst, M., and C. Kelley. (1995). "Collaborating to Improve Children's Services: Politics and Policymaking." In *School-Community Connections: Exploring Issues for Research and Practice*, edited by L.C. Rigsby, M.C. Reynolds, and M.C. Wang. San Francisco, Calif.: Jossey-Bass.

Levy, J.E., and C. Copple. (1989). *Joining Forces: A Report for the First Year*. Alexandria, Va.: National Association of the State Boards of Education.

Lipsky, D.K., and A. Gartner. (1989). *Beyond Separate Education: Quality Education for All*. Baltimore, Md.: Paul H. Brookes.

Massey, D., and N. Denton. (1993). *American Apartheid: Segregation and the Making of the Underclass*. Cambridge, Mass.: Harvard University Press.

McDonnell, L.M., and P.T. Hill. (1993). *Newcomers in American Schools*. Santa Monica, Calif.: Rand Corporation.

Means, R.K., and M.S. Knapp. (1991). *Teaching Advanced Skills to Educationally Disadvantaged Students*. Washington, D.C.: U.S. Department of Education.

National Association of State Boards of Education Study Group on Special Education. (1992). *Winners All: A Call for Inclusive Schools*. Alexandria, Va.: Author.

National Commission on Chapter 1. (1992). *Making Schools Work for Children in Poverty*. Washington, D.C.: Council of Chief State School Officers.

National Commission on Children. (1991). *Beyond Rhetoric: A New American Agenda for Children and Families*. Washington, D.C.: Author.

Noyelle, T., and T. Stanbeck. (1984). *The Economic Transformation of American Cities*. Totowa, N.J.: Rowman and Allanheld.

Oakes, J. (1985). *Keeping Track: How Schools Structure Inequality*. New Haven, Conn.: Yale University Press.

Oberti v. Clementon, 995 F.2d 1204, (3rd Cir. 1993).

Pennsylvania Human Relations Commission v. School District of Philadelphia. (1973, 1994, 1995). 161 Pennsylvania Commonwealth Court 658, 38, A.2d 304.

Pugach, M. (1995). "Twice Victims: The Struggle to Educate Childen in Urban Schools and the Reform of Special Education and Chapter 1." In *Making a Difference for Students At Risk: Trends and Alternatives,* edited by M.C. Wang and M.C. Reynolds. Thousand Oaks, Calif.: Corwin.

Renzulli, J.S., S.M. Reis, T.P. Hebert, and E.I. Diaz. (1995). "The Plight of High-Ability Students in Urban Schools." In *Making a Difference for Students At Risk: Trends and Alternatives,* edited by M.C. Wang and M.C. Reynolds. Thousand Oaks, Calif.: Corwin.

Reynolds, M.C. (1989). *The Knowledge Base for the Beginning Teacher.* Oxford, England: Pergamon Press.

Rigsby, L.C., M.C. Reynolds, and M.C. Wang, eds. (1995). *School-Community Connections: Exploring Issues for Research and Practice.* San Francisco, Calif.: Jossey-Bass.

Schorr, L., and D. Schorr. (1988). *Within Our Reach: Breaking the Cycle of Disadvantage.* New York: Anchor Books.

Tyack, D. (1992). "Health and Social Services in Public Schools: Historical Perspectives." *The Future of Children* 2, 1: 19-31.

U.S. Department of Education. (1994). *The Goals 2000: Educate America Act: A Strategy for Reinventing our Schools.* Washington, D.C.: Author.

U.S. Department of Education. (1995). *Proceedings of the Invitational Conference for Comprehensive School-Linked Services.* Leesburg, Va.: Author.

Wang, M.C. (March 1986). "Educational Segregation: A Civil Rights Concern." Paper presented at the Conference on School Segregation, School District of Philadelphia. Philadelphia, Pa.

Wang, M.C. (1992). *Adaptive Education Strategies: Building on Diversity.* Baltimore: Paul H. Brookes.

Wang, M.C., and E.W. Gordon. (1994). *Educational Resilience in Inner-City America: Challenges and Prospects.* Hillsdale, N.J.: Lawrence Erlbaum.

Wang, M.C., G.D. Haertel, and H.J. Walberg. (1994). "Effective Features of Collaborative School-Linked Services for Children in Elementary Schools: What Do We Know from Research and Practice?" Paper prepared for the Invitational Conference on School-Linked Comprehensive Services for Children and Families, Leesburg, Va.

Wang, M.C., G.D. Haertel, and H.J. Walberg. (1995). "School-Linked Services: A Research Synthesis." In *Changing Populations/ Changing Schools: The Ninety-Fourth Yearbook of the National Society for the Study of Education,* edited by E. Flaxman and A.H. Passow. Chicago: NSSE.

Wang, M.C., J. Oates, and N. Weishew. (1995). "Effective School Responses to Student Diversity in Inner-City Schools: A Coordinated Approach." *Education and Urban Society* 27, 4: 484-503.

Wang, M.C., and M.C. Reynolds, eds. (1995). *Making a Difference for Students At Risk: Trends and Alternatives.* Thousand Oaks, Calif.: Corwin.

Wang, M.C., and M.C. Reynolds. (1994). "Special Education: Accelerated Reforms." Research report to the Office of Educational Research and Improvement, National Center on Education in the Inner Cities, Temple University Center for Research in Human Development and Education.

Will, M.C. (1986). "Educating Children with Learning Problems: A Shared Responsibility." *Exceptional Children* 52, 5: 411-416.

Yancey, W., and S. Saporito. (1994). "Urban Schools and Neighborhoods: A Handbook for Building an Ecological Database." Research report to the Office of Educational Research and Improvement, National Center on Education in the Inner Cities, Temple University Center for Research in Human Development and Education.

Yancey, W., and S. Saporito. (1995). "Ecological Embeddedness of Educational Processes and Outcomes." In *School-Community Connections: Exploring Issues for Research and Practice,* edited by L.C. Rigsby, M.C. Reynolds, and M.C. Wang. San Francisco, Calif.: Jossey-Bass.

3

Cultural Values in Learning and Education

PATRICIA MARKS GREENFIELD, CATHERINE RAEFF,
AND BLANCA QUIROZ

B y the time children enter school, most of them have mastered modes of interpersonal engagement through interactions with their families and communities. Yet U.S. families and communities are culturally diverse, particularly in urban settings. And their customary modes of activity and interaction often differ from those favored by the mainstream Euro-American culture in public schools.

Empirical research generally focuses on how differences in children's cultural backgrounds affect their acquisition of skills in school (Heath 1983). Such studies identify facets of school curriculums that are culturally biased and that contribute to the urban achievement gap. However, reductionist views of development that focus on isolated dimensions—such as the acquisition of specific skills or the design of curriculums based only on cognitive functioning—do not go far enough. It is just as important to recognize that the cultural value systems in which children grow up also influence their development.

In this chapter, we consider how cultural history and values shape developmental goals of immigrant and minority children in the United States and how those values may conflict with the goals and values favored in public schools. We explore two primary value orientations: collectivism and individualism, often termed interdependence and independence (Markus and Kitayama 1991). We begin with a theory about the role of cultural history and cultural values in minority children's development. Next, we review how the cultural value orientations of individualism and collectivism shape children's developing competencies. We follow with concrete examples of how individualism and collectivism can conflict when children of minority, collectivistic cultures encounter individualism in U.S. schools. The chapter ends with implications for schools and teaching practices, models of minority children's education, and a theory for multicultural development.

DEVELOPMENT IN CULTURAL CONTEXTS

Developmental psychology has undergone something of a paradigm shift. A decade ago it isolated the individual's development from various social influences; today it focuses on how varying social interactions affect development (Greenfield 1984, Rogoff 1990, Vygotsky 1978).

According to this view, children develop competencies through social interactions. These social interactions, in turn, reflect cultural values and standards for appropriate behavior. In other words, children's social interactions are culturally constituted. This shift in thinking needs more exploration, particularly in regard to how cultural values shape development and which dimensions of culture may be particularly salient for minority children in U.S. urban schools.

MINORITY CHILD DEVELOPMENT AND CULTURAL HISTORY

Vygotsky highlighted the importance of cultural history as a dimension in understanding individual development within various ethnic groups (Scribner 1985). Ethnic groups grow out of the interaction of a heritage culture with a dominant culture (Kim 1991). Minority research up to now has focused mostly on the contact culture. Less attention has been paid to the culture of origin (Berry 1987). We believe that both aspects of cultural history are a central component of minority children's development.

Different ethnic groups have different perspectives on the role of ancestral cultural history. These perspectives vary with a group's traditions and the time and manner in which the group becomes incorporated into a dominant society. For example, Japanese Americans are at one extreme in the United States, placing so much importance on ancestral history that they call every generation since emigration from Japan by its own distinct name. At another extreme are African Americans, among whom the significance of African roots is quite controversial. One view holds that the experience of slavery and subsequent discrimination entirely wiped out a distinctive African American culture. Yet some practices from that culture remain. For example, African American handclapping games are practically identical to games played in West Africa (Merrill-Mirsky 1991). Sudarkasa (1988) acknowledges the historical influence of slavery, but posits that the prior culture of Africans who adapted to and survived slavery affected the nature of their adaptation.

VALUE ORIENTATIONS: A KEY ASPECT OF CULTURAL HISTORY

Development and socialization take place as people adapt to different ecological and economic conditions (Berry 1967, 1994; Draper and Cashdan 1988). This adaptation accounts for the material side of culture. However, human beings have an intrinsic need to create meaning from their experiences as well (Bruner 1990). How they do so becomes reflected and rationalized in different value orientations. We call this the symbolic side of culture. Kim (1991) brings these two sides together in a view of culture as a collective way to attach meaning to ecological conditions.

The social ecology and economic circumstances of minority children in the United States (or in other Western countries) often differ from those of children growing up in the societies of their ancestral origin. The ways in which these children adapt to ecological conditions (the material side of culture) are less likely to demonstrate their ancestral cultural roots than are their value orientations (an aspect of symbolic culture). Value orientations are the major source of ancestral continuity in minority children's development.

Viewing behavior and thought processes from a values perspective makes it possible to go beyond the mere identification of cultural or other group differences. It enables us to understand the adaptive function and the meaning of cultural differences for the groups involved (Kim and Choi 1994).

THE ACQUISITION OF CULTURE

Culture in this discussion means a group's knowledge and expectations about appropriate modes of interaction and the patterns of activities that are common to that group. As children develop, they construct these modes of appropriate behavior by participating in a variety of social interactions. Interaction in each setting is based on and reflects an "invisible culture" (Phillips 1972). Invisible culture involves the implicit communication of values, norms, and aspirations through social interaction and every day routines (Cazden 1988).

Children come to school acting in accordance with the invisible cultures of their homes and communities. Conflict arises when their behavior differs from the invisible culture of the school. The school may sometimes devalue and even punish, albeit inadvertently, children for behavior that their parents value. Because the cultures are invisible, such conflicts often are not even recognized as cultural. Ironically, teachers may conscientiously try to create culturally sensitive environments for their students (e.g., through multicultural displays and activities) while simultaneously structuring classroom interaction patterns that violate invisible cultural norms of various minority groups. Teachers also may inadvertently criticize parents for adhering to a different set of ideals about children, families, and parenting.

INDIVIDUALISM AND COLLECTIVISM

Recent theory and research have distinguished the cultural value orientation of individualism and collectivism (e.g., Greenfield and Cocking 1994, Kagitcibasi 1989, Triandis 1989). Harking back to its Anglo-Saxon and European immigrant origins, mainstream culture in the United States is generally individualistic (Lebra 1994). It encourages independence and individual achievement as important goals of development (Markus and Kitayama 1991). The public school system is one cultural-institutional setting that highlights these aspects of individualism.

In contrast, many non-Western immigrant and minority groups now living in urban areas of the United States have a cultural history of collectivism. Collectivism is a cultural value orientation that emphasizes interdependence as well as the preservation and permanence of prescribed relationships that are hierarchically structured around family roles and multiple generations. This history is part of the cultural and cross-cultural roots of Native Americans, Latin Americans, Africans, and Asians (Greenfield and Cocking 1994).

With different developmental goals that are shaped by different patterns of social interaction, children from individualistic and collectivistic value orientations become adept at different modes of activity, and they have different conceptions of appropriate behavior.

PRESCHOOL SOCIALIZATION OF INDIVIDUALISM AND COLLECTIVISM

Conceptualizations of intelligence in individualistic and collectivistic cultures differ. In collectivistic cultures, infants spend most of their time with other human beings. The value of physical objects is primarily that they mediate social relationships, as gifts do, for example (Greenfield, Brazelton, and Childs 1989; Rabain-Jamin 1994). Individualistic cultures, on the other hand, tend to emphasize technological knowledge of the physical world as a way of facilitating independence. Parents are likely to hope and believe that their children will be verbally competent and able to construct knowledge of the physical world from observing and manipulating toys that stimulate independence. To that end, a parent in the United States might provide a baby with toys so that the baby will amuse himself or herself and not require constant attention. Similarly, parents in individualistic cultures tend to emphasize distal modes of communication through linguistic means, as opposed to proximal modes of communication such as touching and holding (Greenfield 1994).

Because knowledge of the physical world and linguistic communication by and large define children's early cognitive development, parents from independence-oriented, individualistic cultures place a high value on them. In contrast, parents from interdependence-oriented cultures are likely to promote their children's social intelligence.

INDIVIDUALISM VERSUS COLLECTIVISM AND THE SCHOOLS

Schools in the United States emphasize individualism and independence as a goal of development. Many classroom interactions and activities aim for individual achievement, encourage autonomous choice and initiative, and develop logico-rational cognitive skills (Delgado-Gaitan 1993, 1994). Unless part of socially structured and identified collaborative activities, cooperation in school activities is called "cheating" (Whiting and Whiting 1973, 1994). Student evaluations are based on independent work.

These characteristics of schooling contrast with the collectivistic traditions of many minority and immigrant cultures in urban schools (e.g., Hispanic, Asian American, Native American, and African American). The ancestral cultures of these groups emphasize interpersonal relationships, respect for elders and tradition, responsibility for others, and cooperation (Blake 1993, 1994; Delgado-Gaitan 1993, 1994; Ho 1994; Kim and Choi 1994; Suina and Smolkin 1994).

Encouraging children's individual achievements in school can stimulate an independent sense of self that undermines a sense of self based on social affiliation and responsibility for others. For example, hierarchical relationships and respect for elders and authority are important elements in collectivistic cultures (Triandis 1989). They contrast with the individualistic view of egalitarianism. However, the development of critical thinking requires children to articulate and even argue their views with older family members on a relatively egalitarian basis (Delgado-Gaitan 1993, 1994). This practice can become a source of conflict between these two value orientations because the academic performance of children who are not vocal and adept at logico-rational modes of argumentation is likely to be evaluated negatively.

In addition, the impersonal text rather than the knowledge and wisdom of older family members is the basic source of learning in U.S. schools. But in the Pueblo Indian world view, for example, parents and grandparents are the repositories of knowledge. This provides a social connection between the generations. The introduction of encyclopedias, reference books, and the like undermines "the very fiber of the connectedness" (Suina 1991, p. 153). Along with teachers, such books displace family elders as the authorities for knowledge. Collectivistic or interdependence-oriented societies, such as in Japan and China, adhere to strong collectivistic practices in their classrooms, including learning from other children and teaching the whole class rather than attending to individual students (Stigler and Perry 1988). These practices moderate the individualistic bias intrinsic to school-based formal education.

CONFLICTS BETWEEN INDIVIDUALISM AND COLLECTIVISM IN THE SCHOOLS

Conflicts between individualism and collectivism play out in urban school settings, often without the teacher being aware of it. A real-life incident from Los Angeles serves as an example. A preschool boy is playing with a toy. A girl, the daughter of Mexican immigrant parents, takes the toy to play with it. The boy hits her. The teacher's response is to tell the girl that she should not take other children's toys. The Mexican American mother, looking on, becomes upset that the teacher did not reprimand the boy for his act of aggression. After all, this mother commented, in her extended family, material objects are shared. Possession or personal property is a negative concept akin to selfishness. Her interpretation of the incident comes from her collectivistic view: The boy showed selfishness in refusing to share the toy with her daughter, and then he compounded his undesirable behavior with physical aggression.

In contrast, the teacher's reaction is consonant with individualistic values of independence. Objects are the property of a single individual, even if only temporarily, as in school. Hence, the teacher treats the girl as the primary transgressor because she took away a toy "belonging" to another child. Clearly not all teachers from the mainstream U.S. culture would respond as this teacher did. Many would focus on the undesirability of physical aggression. But, those with an individualistic orientation—and its valuing of private property—would probably see the boy as the original victim and the girl as the first encroacher. Because the girl would not be seen as a victim of the boy's selfishness, her own legitimate need for rectification would go unrecognized.

If the teacher and the parent were familiar with each other's value systems, dialogue and compromise on how to respond to such incidents would be possible. However, with no understanding of the other party's value system, misunderstanding and frustration are likely to result, forcing the child to struggle with mixed messages about social behavior. The implication for education is that teachers and parents need to understand and respect each other's value systems, and they should seek ways to harmonize them for the benefit of children, families, classrooms, and communities.

Other examples of conflicts between individualism and collectivism exist as well. A teacher in Los Angeles described a situation in which Hispanic students formed groups at every opportunity, despite the teacher's insistence that students work alone. The primary purpose of these groups was not necessarily to work on the task together but simply to be together and to talk while working. However, from the teacher's point of view, this social interaction was a problem, if not outright cheating.

During one of our observations of a Los Angeles prekindergarten class made up of mostly Hispanic children, the teacher was showing a real chicken egg that would soon hatch. While teaching the physical properties of the egg, she asked children to describe eggs by thinking about the times they had cooked and eaten them. One child tried three times to talk about how she cooked eggs with her grandmother, but the teacher disregarded these comments in favor of a child who explained that the insides of eggs are white and yellow. The Hispanic member of our research team noted that the first child's answer was typical of the associations that her invisible home culture encourages. That is, objects are most meaningful when they mediate social interactions. But in this case, the teacher expected students to describe eggs as isolated physical entities. Eggs as mediators of social relationships and behavior were irrelevant.

This incident has a number of implications for urban education. First, because she did not even see the invisible culture that generated the description of cooking eggs with grandmother, the teacher devalued the child's contribution and, implicitly, the value orientation it reflected. Second, because she did not consider the collectivistic value orientation, she did not realize that her question was ambiguous. Children who share the teacher's value orientation will assume she is interested in the physical properties of eggs, even though she has not explicitly said so. Those children who do not share the teacher's value orientation will assume differently. In a culturally sensitive school environment, the teacher both validates the social relationships of children from collectivistic backgrounds by showing interest in their family experiences and is explicit about her expectations for a topic of study. This approach facilitates a process of bidirectional cultural exchange at school: Some collectivistic values become part of the classroom while, at the same time, children from collectivist cultures get practice in the cognitive operations necessary for school success.

The different value placed on cognitive and social development was again illustrated during conferences between a teacher and Hispanic immigrant parents of 4th graders. To the teacher, the conference was a forum for discussing the children's academic performance—the children as independent achievers with unique capabilities and potential. In contrast, parents wanted to talk about their children's social behavior and role in the family. The result was miscommunication and frustration on both sides. Neither party seemed to be aware, however, that the frustration and dissatisfaction stemmed from fundamental differences in their views of the children themselves. That is, the teacher saw the children as independent learners, but to parents they were family members. Mutual understanding of invisible cultures could open up dialogue about both cultural views.

A final example of conflict between individualism and collectivism demonstrates the struggle immigrant Hispanic families are going through as they try to reconcile their collectivistic home cultures with the individualistic orientation of the public schools. In this study, we analyzed how children, parents, and teachers respond to scenarios of interpersonal situations that may occur in home and school settings (Raeff, Greenfield, and Quiroz in press). Each scenario involved an interpersonal dilemma that could be solved individualistically or collectivistically. Analyses of pilot data indicate that teachers responded overwhelmingly individualistically (80 percent), whereas Hispanic immigrant mothers responded collectivistically almost all of the time

(90 percent). Hispanic children responded in between the two, with an average of 64 percent collectivistic responses. Let us illustrate with the following scenario.

Erica tells her mother that she got the highest grade in the class on her math test. She says she is really proud of herself for doing so well and for doing the best in the class. She says she guesses she is really smart. When asked how the mother should respond, a teacher said: "Agree emphatically that 'yes' she certainly is smart and that the test proves that she is capable of doing virtually anything if she applies herself. Erica has done well and needs the appropriate recognition. It will obviously enhance self-esteem and increase her chances of success in life." In contrast, an Hispanic immigrant mother answered, "She should congratulate her, but tell her not to praise herself too much. She should not think so much of herself." Moreover, this mother worried that too much praise could make the student see other children as less worthy.

This example demonstrates the teacher's view of the child as a self-contained, independent achiever. As far as the teacher is concerned, there is no conflict in this scenario because if the student did her best on the test, she is entitled to feel proud of herself. However, the mother perceived a conflict; namely, the student deserved credit for doing well but she should not separate her achievement from her relationship to the group. An implication for educational practice is the need to incorporate both cultural orientations into criterion-referenced tests. That would allow the whole group to meet a standard instead of making one child's gain in academic achievement another child's loss, as is the case in curved assessments.

HISTORICAL POWER RELATIONSHIPS BETWEEN MAJORITY AND MINORITY GROUPS

Ancestral roots are only one part of minority children's culture. Ogbu (1993, 1994) points out that minority children must also cope with another important factor in their development: the history and nature of power relationships between minority and majority cultures.

Minority groups fall into two major classifications: involuntary minority groups (those who become incorporated into a nation through conquest, slavery, or colonization) and voluntary minority groups (those who become incorporated into a nation through voluntary immigration). Involuntary groups tend to oppose the cultural values of the majority (Ogbu 1993, 1994) to keep the conquerors, enslavers, and colonizers from wiping out their indigenous cultures. They feel they cannot adopt any of the ways of the majority without giving up parts of their own culture. Involuntary minorities differ from voluntary minorities in that the societies to which voluntary minorities immigrate generally tolerate their culture. African Americans (through slavery), Native Americans (through conquest) and, to some extent, Mexican Americans (through conquest of the U.S. Southwest from Mexico) are classified as involuntary minorities (Ogbu 1994). Involuntary minorities see schools as majority institutions. Therefore, academic achievement challenges their group loyalties and ethnic identities.

Voluntary minorities are secure in their ethnic identities, but they want to learn new ways that will enable them to succeed in their new country (Ogbu 1994). For them, schooling is a new way that leads to opportunity. Asian Americans constitute voluntary minorities; they use schooling as a path to achievement in the broader society. Unlike the experience of involuntary minorities—such as African Americans, Native Americans, and Mexican Americans—the dominant culture has never actively tried to eradicate the culture and language of voluntary immigrants.

Because U.S. society has actively attempted to eradicate the culture of every involuntary minority group, involuntary minorities find historical justification for believing that their ancestral or ethnic culture and Euro-American culture, including its schools, are mutually exclusive. For example, Native American children were forcibly put into government boarding schools whose major goal was to eradicate Native American culture and languages. For this reason, the most successful schooling for Native Americans has been in their own community-run institutions. Being separate from, and even opposing, the dominant culture are important for involuntary minorities to retain their culture.

The bottom line is that the cultural history of minority groups creates two kinds of value diversity that are relevant to urban education. The first is the diversity of values that comes from the various ancestral cultures that make up the United States. The second is the diversity of values that comes from the various ways in which groups become part of our nation, the values that are a function of the history of relations between minority groups and the wider society (Ogbu 1993, 1994). Urban education can benefit by expanding its efforts to take both kinds of value diversity into account.

IMPLICATIONS FOR EDUCATIONAL PRACTICE

Acquiring more knowledge about the cultural roots of involuntary minorities by minorities themselves, as well as by members of the dominant society, is one step toward recognizing positive bicultural identities. Schools should encourage and help urban children from involuntary minority groups explore their ancestral cultural roots so that they can develop a positive cultural identity. Positive identities can ultimately replace the cultural conflicts that hold so much power over involuntary minority children in urban areas.

It is also important for the mental health of voluntary minorities that schools help maintain pride in their culture of origin, as Kim and Choi (1994) demonstrate for Korean Americans and Korean Canadians. When pressure from an individualistic environment leads people from collectivist cultures to surrender their way of living and child rearing, what is the psychological price? This question has only recently received attention because educational research and practice have generally been from the perspective of the dominant society.

Our ultimate goal in examining how individualism and collectivism differentially shape children's learning and socialization is to influence classroom practices and school policies toward urban families and communities. We want to encourage schools to better understand and appreciate the modes of behavior that children bring to the classroom from their invisible home and community cultures. Just acknowledging the existence of another culture validates it. School may be less threatening to minority parents, particularly immigrant parents, if they feel there is some attempt to validate and understand their values.

Recognizing the positive sources of learning and cognitive development in diverse cultural groups can help schools to appreciate, utilize, and adapt to the strengths that minority children bring with them into the classroom. Increasing their knowledge about cultural history will enable members of the dominant society to understand and appreciate the distinctive styles of cognitive socialization and learning of minority children and vice versa. This knowledge would open up communication between schools and homes and ultimately benefit parents, teachers, and, particularly, students.

The most constructive approach for schools may be to accommodate select socialization practices and values from children's home and community cultures (Tharp and Gallimore 1988). Such a cultural compatibility model stresses the simultaneous promotion of children's home/community cultures and adjustment to the mainstream culture. We further suggest that classroom practices that include both minority culture and mainstream U.S. culture can benefit all children, majority as well as minority, in terms of learning, social behavior, attitudes, and classroom climate (Kagan 1986). In more general terms, an understanding of cultural roots creates pride in oneself and one's group, as well as appreciation of other groups. Indeed, this is the significance of Jesse Jackson's suggestion that the term "black" be replaced by "African American." The latter emphasizes the influence of African roots on black psychology and society (Njeri 1989).

One specific intervention is to gear teacher workshops toward expanding the values of interdependence and responsibility for others. This would help teachers of urban minority or immigrant children make their students feel that they are part of their school community. Another method might be to establish day-care centers for preschool children in elementary schools so that elementary children can help as caregivers. Such activities could develop a sense of social responsibility in the young caregivers (Whiting and Whiting 1994). Such interventions would also test the idea that all children, not just immigrant or minority children, benefit from a better balance between social responsibility and independence in school.

Continuing efforts to create a feedback loop that involves parents, students, and teachers is an important strategy. Many parents, as well as teachers, may not know that children's success in school partly depends on their ability to master modes of activity and interaction that are very different from and may even conflict with value orientations that are emphasized at home. Collectivistic-oriented parents may perceive the school's emphasis on developing each child's potential as encouraging undesirable selfishness. When the collectivistic or interdependence-oriented immigrant parent keeps a child home from school to help take care of a sick baby, he or she sees the child as both learning and enacting a responsible prosocial role. In contrast, the school, with its individualistic perspective, sees the parent as interfering with the child's independent educational development. Parents and teachers must continue to work together to find strategies to incorporate and encourage individually oriented school achievement and development while maintaining valued forms of interdependence, such as family unity, aid, and sharing. For parents, as well as teachers, to know about each other's expectations facilitates communication and enables urban parents from collectivistic cultures to participate more actively in the schools.

TOWARD A MULTICULTURAL MODEL OF DEVELOPMENT

The implications of developmental and educational theory by and large revolve around one major theme: The need to recognize that patterns and norms of development and education previously thought to be universal are often specific to Euro-American culture, and Euro-American culture is the culture of the schools. We hope that further understanding of the historical roots that influence minority children's development will help urban educators move away from a model of minority children's development that views differences as deficiencies (Cole and Bruner 1971) and beyond a coping model of minority children's development that sees differences simply as adaptations to unfavorable conditions in the dominant society (McLloyd 1990, Ogbu 1994). Even more fundamental for educators is a diversity model (Cole and Bruner 1971, Rogoff and Morelli 1989) that recognizes that learning differences are rooted in historic cultural values that, instead of being assimilated out of existence, can make an important contribution to a diverse society.

The U.S. ideal of the self-fulfilled individual has turned into an extreme of widespread isolation, alienation, and violence. An emphasis on family responsibility and solidarity so intrinsic to collectivist cultures can infuse a moderating influence of great importance in our society.

ENDNOTE

We would like to thank The University of California at Los Angeles, Urban Education Studies Center, for their grant support on this project. We would also like to recognize our teacher collaborators, Marie Altchech and Ana Serrano, for their invaluable roles as consultants and site facilitators for this project, as well as the wonderful job of our research assistants Patricia Morales, Hedwig Woelfl, Claudia Torres, Rachel Ostroy, Mirella Benitez, and Kenichi Sakai. We also express our most sincere appreciation to Stoner Avenue Elementary School and Corinne A. Seeds University Elementary School for their cooperation.

REFERENCES

Berry, J.W. (1967). "Independence and Conformity in Subsistence-Level Societies." *Journal of Personality and Social Psychology* 7, 4: 415-418.

Berry, J.W. (August 1987). "Ecological Analyses for Acculturation Research." Paper presented at the International Association for Cross-Cultural Psychology, Newcastle, Australia.

Berry, J.W. (1994). "An Ecological Perspective on Cultural and Ethnic Psychology." In *Human Diversity: Perspectives on People in Context*, edited by E. Trickett, R. Watts, and D. Birman. San Francisco, Calif.: Jossey-Bass.

Blake, I.K. (1993). "Learning Language in Context: The Social-Emotional Orientation of African American Mother-Child Communication." *International Journal of Behavioral Development* 16, 3: 443-464.

Blake, I.K. (1994). "Language Development and Socialization in Young African-American Children." In *Cross-Cultural Roots of Minority Child Development*, edited by P.M. Greenfield and R.R. Cocking. Hillsdale, N.J.: Lawrence Erlbaum.

Bruner, J.S. (1990). *Acts of Meaning*. Cambridge, Mass.: Harvard University.

Cazden, C.B. (1988). *Classroom Discourse: The Language of Teaching and Learning.* Portsmouth, N.H.: Heinemann.

Cole, M., and J.S. Bruner. (1971). "Cultural Differences and Inferences about Psychological Processes." *American Psychologist* 26, 10: 867-876.

Delgado-Gaitan, C. (1993). "Parenting in Two Generations of Mexican American Families." *International Journal of Behavioral Development* 16, 3: 409-427.

Delgado-Gaitan, C. (1994). "Socializing Young Children in Mexican American Families: An Intergenerational Perspective." In *Cross-Cultural Roots of Minority Child Development*, edited by P.M. Greenfield and R.R. Cocking. Hillsdale, N.J.: Lawrence Erlbaum.

Draper, P., and E. Cashdan. (1988). "Technological Change and Child Behavior Among the !Kung." *Ethnology* 27: 339-365.

Greenfield, P.M. (1994). "Independence and Interdependence as Developmental Script: Implications for Theory, Research, and Practice." In *Cross-Cultural Roots of Minority Child Development*, edited by P.M. Greenfield and R.R. Cocking. Hillsdale: N.J.: Lawrence Erlbaum.

Greenfield, P.M. (1984). "A Theory of the Teacher in the Learning Activities of Everyday Life." In *Everyday Cognition: Its Development in Social Context*, edited by B. Rogoff and J. Lave. Cambridge, Mass.: Harvard University.

Greenfield, P.M., T.B. Brazelton, and C. Childs. (1989). "From Birth to Maturity in Zinacantan: Ontogenesis in Cultural Context." In *Ethnographic Encounters in Southern Mesoamerica: Celebratory Essays in Honor of Evon Z. Vogt*, edited by V. Bricker and G. Gossen. Albany, N.Y.: Institute of Mesoamerican Studies, State University of New York.

Greenfield, P.M., and R.R. Cocking. (1994). *Cross-Cultural Roots of Minority Child Development.* Hillsdale, N.J.: Lawrence Erlbaum.

Heath, S.B. (1983). *Ways with Words.* Cambridge, Mass.: Cambridge University.

Ho, D.Y.F. (1994). "Cognitive Socialization in Confucian Heritage Cultures." In *Cross-Cultural Roots of Minority Child Development*, edited by P.M. Greenfield and R.R. Cocking. Hillsdale, N.J.: Lawrence Erlbaum.

Kagan, S. (1986). "Cooperative Learning and Sociocultural Factors in Schooling." In *Beyond Language: Social and Cultural Factors in Schooling Language Minority Students.* Los Angeles, Calif.: Evaluation, Dissemination, and Assessment Center.

Kagitcibasi, C. (1989). "Approaches to Studying the Family and Socialization." *Nebraska Symposium on Motivation* 37: 135- 200.

Kim, U. (June/July 1991). "Discussion." In *Continuities and Discontinuities in the Cognitive Socialization of Minority Children,* chaired by P.M. Greenfield and R.R. Cocking. Proceedings of a workshop, Department of Health and Human Services, Public Health Service, Alcohol, Drug Abuse and Mental Health Administration, Washington, D.C.

Kim, U., and S.H. Choi. (1994). "Individualism, Collectivism, and Child Development: A Korean Perspective." In *Cross-Cultural Roots of Minority Child Development,* edited by P.M. Greenfield and R.R. Cocking. Hillsdale, N.J.: Lawrence Erlbaum.

Lebra, T.S. (1994). "Mother and Child in a Japanese Socialization: A Japan-U.S. Comparison." In *Cross-Cultural Roots of Minority Child Development,* edited by P.M. Greenfield and R.R. Cocking. Hillsdale, N.J.: Lawrence Erlbaum.

Markus, H.R., and S. Kitayama. (1991). "Culture and the Self: Implications for Cognition, Emotion, and Motivation." *Psychological Review* 98, 2: 242-253.

McLloyd, V.C. (1990). "The Impact of Economic Hardship on Black Families and Children: Psychological Distress, Parenting, and Socioemotional Development." *Child Development* 61, 2: 311-346.

Merrill-Mirsky, C. (June/July 1991). "Eeny Meeny Pepsadeeny: Ethnicity and Gender in Children's Musical Play." In "Continuities and Discontinuities in the Cognitive Socialization of Minority Children," chaired by P.M. Greenfield and R.R. Cocking. Proceedings of a workshop, Department of Health and Human Services, Public Health Service, Alcohol, Drug Abuse and Mental Health Administration, Washington, D.C.

Njeri, I. (January 29, 1989). "What's in a Name? African-American is the Accurate Ethnic Label of the Past and the Future, Black Leaders Say." *Los Angeles Times,* p. VI-1.

Ogbu, J.U. (1993). "Differences in Cultural Frame of Reference." *International Journal of Behavioral Development* 16, 3: 483-506.

Ogbu, J.U. (1994). "From Cultural Differences to Differences in Cultural Frame of Reference." In *Cross Cultural Roots of Minority Child Development,* edited by P.M. Greenfield and R.R. Cocking. Hillsdale, N.J.: Lawrence Erlbaum.

Phillips, S.U. (1972). "Participant Structures and Communicative Competence: Wann Springs Children in Community and Classroom." In *Functions of Language in the Classroom,* edited by C.B. Cazden, V.P.

John, and D. Hymes. New York: Teachers College.

Rabain-Jamin, J. (1994). "Language and Socialization of the Child in African Families Living in France. In *Cross Cultural Roots of Minority Child Development*, edited by P.M. Greenfield and R.R. Cocking. Hillsdale, N.J.: Lawrence Erlbaum.

Raeff, C., P.M. Greenfield, and B. Quiroz, (in press). "Conceptualizing Interpersonal Relationships in the Cultural Contexts of Individualism and Collectivism." *New Directions in Child Development.* San Francisco: Jossey-Bass.

Rogoff, B. (1990). *Apprenticeship in Thinking.* New York: Oxford University Press.

Rogoff, B., and G. Morelli. (1989). "Perspectives on Children's Development from Cultural Psychology." *American Psychologist* 44, 2: 343-348.

Scribner, S. (1985). "Vygotsky's Uses of History." In *Culture, Communication and Cognition: Vygotskian Perspectives*, edited by J.V. Wertsch. New York: Cambridge University.

Stigler, J.W., and M. Perry. (1988). "Mathematics Learning in Japanese, Chinese, and American Classrooms." In *Children's Mathematics. New Directions for Child Development, No. 41.*, edited by G.B. Saxe and M. Gearhart. San Francisco: Jossey-Bass.

Sudarkasa, N. (1988). "Interpreting the African Heritage in Afro-American Family Organization." In *Black Families*, edited by H.P. McAdoo. Newbury Park, Calif.: Sage.

Suina, J.H. (June/July 1991). "Discussion." In *Continuities and Discontinuities in the Cognitive Socialization of Minority Children*, chaired by P.M. Greenfield and R.R. Cocking. Proceedings of a workshop, Department of Health and Human Services, Public Health Service, Alcohol, Drug Abuse and Mental Health Administration, Washington, D.C.

Suina, J.H., and L.B. Smolkin. (1994). "From Natal Culture to School Culture to Dominant Society Culture: Supporting Transitions for Pueblo Indian Students." In *Cross Cultural Roots of Minority Child Development*, edited by P.M. Greenfield and R.R. Cocking. Hillsdale, N.J.: Lawrence Erlbaum.

Tharp, R.G., and R. Gallimore. (1988). *Rousing Minds to Life: Teaching, Learning and Schooling in Social Context.* Cambridge, Mass.: Cambridge University.

Triandis, H.C. (1989). "Cross Cultural Studies of Individualism and Collectivism." *Nebraska Symposium on Motivation* 37: 41-133.

Vygotsky, L.S. (1978). *Mind in Society.* Cambridge, Mass.: Harvard University Press.

Whiting, J.W.M., and B.B. Whiting. (1973). "Altruistic and Egoistic Behavior in Six Cultures." In *Cultural Illness and Health: Essays in Human Adaptation,* edited by L. Nader and T.W. Maretzki. Washington, D.C.: American Anthropological Association.

Whiting, J.W.M., and B.B. Whiting. (1994). "Altruistic and Egoistic Behavior in Six Cultures." In *Culture and Human Development,* edited by E.H. Chasdi. New York: Cambridge University.

4

Educating Teachers to Close the Achievement Gap: Issues of Pedagogy, Knowledge, and Teacher Preparation

Kenneth M. Zeichner

Numerous approaches to curriculum and instruction can help close the achievement gap between poor children of color and their middle class peers. However, no approach will work without corresponding changes in teacher education. This chapter reviews the research literature on what teachers need to be like, to know, and to be able to do to successfully teach poor students of color to high academic standards. It also considers the kinds of changes that must take place in teacher education to support new directions for teaching, learning, and curriculum in urban schools.

TEACHING ALL STUDENTS TO HIGH ACADEMIC STANDARDS: THE RESEARCH LITERATURE

In recent years, research has drawn a clear picture of the kind of teaching, curriculum, and classroom environment that enables all students to achieve high standards. A significant proportion of this research focuses on poor students of color, whom our public schools have traditionally underserved. The key elements that this literature addresses are high expectations for all students, cultural congruence in instruction, teacher knowledge, and teaching strategies.

HIGH EXPECTATIONS FOR ALL STUDENTS

The first element common to effective teachers in urban schools is the belief that all students can be successful learners and the communication of this belief to students (Delpit 1988; Lucas, Henze, and Donato 1990; Quality Education for Minorities Project 1990). These teachers have a personal commitment to helping all students achieve success, and they truly believe that they can make a difference in their students' achievement (Hodge 1990). Winfield (1986) distinguishes between teachers who assume responsibility for their students' learning and those who shift responsibility when students fail to factors such as the students themselves, school bureaucracies, parents, and communities.

The literature is clear about the importance of creating a classroom context in which all students feel valued and capable of academic success. For example, in her studies of successful teachers of African American students, Ladson-Billings (1990) describes some of the ways in which teachers' beliefs about the ability of all of their students to succeed were communicated to the students.

> As I talked with and observed all of the teachers in the study, I was astounded at their constant faith in their students. Even when they scolded the students, the teachers would remark "You're too smart to be doing that," or "You cannot convince me that you're not worth the effort" (p. 23).

Despite evidence to the contrary, many students in teacher education institutions continue to cling to the belief that some students cannot learn, and thus they hold low expectations for them (Goodlad

1990). As Goodlad writes:

> The idea of moral imperatives for teachers was virtually foreign in concept and strange in language for most of the future teachers we interviewed. Many were less than convinced that all students can learn; they voiced the view that they should be kind and considerate to all, but they accepted as fact the theory that some simply cannot learn (p. 264).

Low expectations for student behavior and academic achievement often focus on poor students of color. Research clearly shows that teacher education students, who are mostly white and monolingual, tend to view diversity of student backgrounds as a problem rather than as a resource that enriches teaching and learning. Moreover, many of these future teachers have negative attitudes about racial, ethnic, and language groups other than their own (Law and Lane 1987, Paine 1989). Such attitudes manifest themselves in low expectations, which then are expressed in watered down and fragmented curriculum for poor students (Moll 1988, Nieto 1992, Oakes 1985). Teachers with high expectations for all students, on the other hand, effectively translate their beliefs into a more academically demanding curriculum.

For example, Luis Moll (1988), in describing the elements that contribute to Latino students' school success, is very clear about the curricular shift that needs to accompany high expectations:

> In contrast to the assumption that working class children cannot handle an academically rigorous curriculum, or in the case of limited-English proficient students, that their lack of English fluency justifies an emphasis on low level skills, the guiding assumption in the classrooms analyzed seemed to be the opposite: that students are as smart as allowed by the curriculum. The teachers assumed that the children were competent and capable and that it was the teacher's responsibility to provide the students with a challenging, innovative, and intellectually rigorous curriculum (p. 467).

CULTURAL CONGRUENCE IN INSTRUCTION

It is not enough, however, to make the curriculum more rigorous. The literature is clear about the need for some type of scaffolding or bridge between the cultures of the school and the home in order to teach all students to high academic standards.

Scaffolding consists of constructing a set of supports that enables students to relate school to experiences at home and vice-versa (Mehan and Trujillo 1989). The literature sometimes calls such supports "cultural synchronization" (Irvine 1989). The point is to make curriculum and instruction congruent with what is important to students in their home cultures.

There are many different ways to relate school and home experiences, including the use of teaching strategies such as sheltered bilingual education (Watson, Northcutt, and Rydell 1989) and assisted teaching (Tharp and Gallimore 1988). Reorganizing lesson formats, discourse patterns, behavior standards, curriculum materials, and assessment practices can make them more sensitive to linguistic and cultural variations (Cole and Griffin 1987, Cummins 1986, Garcia 1993, Olsen and Mullen 1990, Strickland and Ascher 1992).

Culturally congruent instruction contains two critical elements: incorporation of students' languages and cultures, and explicit instruction regarding the school's codes and customs.

Incorporating students' languages and cultures into the academic and social context of schooling. Effective teachers understand the cultures of students in their classrooms and adapt curriculum and instruction accordingly. Cultural congruence supports academic learning and helps students identify with and maintain pride in their home cultures (Cummins 1986, 1989; Hollins and Spencer 1990). In culturally congruent classrooms, students can apply language and task completion skills that are already in their repertoires to new learning (Cole and Griffin 1987) by, for example, using their knowledge of Spanish to learn to read English texts (Au and Kawakami 1994).

Other examples of restructuring classroom practices around the cultural resources that students bring to school include the organization of instruction to build upon rules of discourse in the home and community cultures. An example of this approach is the use of peer learning centers and turn-taking in reading groups in classrooms with native Hawaiian children (Tharp and Gallimore 1988). Other restructuring practices noted in the literature are the incorporation of community-related themes into classroom writing projects (Moll and

Diaz 1987) and employing interaction patterns such as choral and responsive reading commonly found in African American churches in classrooms with many African American students (Hollins 1982).

One other very interesting example of the incorporation of cultural content from the community into the classroom is a project directed by Luis Moll at the University of Arizona, which has sought to develop innovations in teaching that draw upon the knowledge and skills found in local households in Mexican American communities in Tucson (Moll, Amanti, Neff, and Gonzalez 1992).

Moll and his colleagues argue that mobilizing "funds of knowledge" in the community for classroom instruction represents a more positive and realistic view of households as containing many cultural and cognitive resources with great potential use for classroom instruction. They have developed an approach that includes training teachers in methods of qualitative research and systematic gathering of information about community knowledge and the social networks that enable this knowledge to be used.

In the particular Mexican American communities that Moll and the teachers have studied, funds of knowledge include such things as farming, carpentry, construction, herbal medicine, child care, midwifery, and cooking. Moll and his colleagues have presented several case studies of how teachers have developed classroom practices that use the community funds of knowledge. These include asking students to write about topics in community living (e.g., construction); developing theme studies based on activities in the community (e.g., the making of traditional Mexican candy); and using parents' expertise in instructional situations (Moll and Greenberg 1990, Moll et. al. 1992, Moll 1992).

Explicitly teaching the school's codes and customs (e.g., the culture of the classroom) allows students to fully participate in the mainstream or "culture of power" (Delpit 1986, 1988; Villegas 1991). Knapp and Turnbull (1991) succinctly capture this principle of cultural congruence in their synthesis of factors associated with school success for poor children. They argue that poor children will be able to better meet academic challenges if schools abide by the following principles:

Teachers know and respect the students' cultural/linguistic backgrounds and communicate this respect in a personal way to the students. The academic program allows and encourages students to draw and build on experiences they have, at the same time it exposes them to unfamiliar experiences and ways of thinking. The assumptions, expectations, and ways of doing things in school—in short, its culture—are made explicit to the students by teachers as they explain and model these dimensions of academic learning (p. 334).

Maintaining students' ethnocultural identities while, simultaneously, familiarizing them with the codes of power requires teachers to combine culturally congruent and consciously incongruent teaching and curriculum strategies (Singer 1988). Because so many elements of cultural variation are present in classrooms, total cultural congruence in instruction is impossible (Bloch and Tabachnick 1991). Teachers can, however, incorporate culture and language-sensitive practices into instruction in their classrooms so that students feel there is respect for their cultural roots (Nieto 1992).

TEACHER KNOWLEDGE

For teachers to implement the principle of cultural congruence, they must have knowledge of and respect for the various cultural traditions and languages of students in their classrooms. Anything less ensures that many ethnic and language minority students will continue to fall short of meeting high academic standards. Teachers need general sociocultural knowledge about child and adolescent development; about second language acquisition (Leighton, Hightower, Wingley, Pechman, and McCollum 1994); and about the ways that socioeconomic circumstances, language, and culture shape school performance (Cazden and Mehan 1990, Comer 1988, Hodge 1990). Finally, according to some (Banks 1991, Hollins 1990), teachers need a clear sense of their own ethnic and cultural identities so they can understand and appreciate those of their students. They also need to become more aware of how their own cultural biases may influence their judgments about student performance and obstruct their students' ability to learn (Bowers and Flinders 1990).

The literature discusses at length the importance of giving teachers information about the values, practices, and learning styles of particular cultural groups (Coballes-Vega 1992). However, there is a risk in this strategy. The concern is that general knowledge about cultural group characteristics may strengthen stereotypes that teachers already hold (McDiarmid and Price 1990). One way to circumvent this is to teach teachers how to learn about and then incorporate into instruction information about their own students, their families, and communities (Cazden and Mehan 1990, Trueba 1989). Teachers can use any number of strategies to acquire information about the various cultures in their classrooms, including "making home visits, conferring with community members, talking with parents, consulting with other teachers, and observing children in and out of school" (Villegas 1993, p. 7).

Teachers, who essentially become researchers of their students and their students' communities (Heath 1983, McCaleb 1995), then adjust their classroom practices to make the local cultural community the baseline for curriculum and instruction. Garcia (1993) identifies three ways in which successful teachers of culturally and linguistically diverse students do this:

• by using cultural referents in both verbal and nonverbal forms to communicate instructional and institutional demands,

• by organizing instruction to build on rules of discourse from the home and community cultures, and

• by showing equal respect to the values and norms of the home and community cultures and those of the school culture.

TEACHING STRATEGIES

Methods of instruction that appear to work most successfully with poor ethnic and language minority students tend to focus on making meaning out of content. This is the exact opposite of the decontextualized skills that schools most often teach these students (Moll 1988). Recent research (Knapp and Shields 1990) challenges the notion that teacher-directed instruction of a skills-based and sequentially ordered curriculum develops students' analytic and conceptual skills and their ability to express themselves in writing. Research attributes the failure of this approach in urban schools to teachers not providing students with a larger meaning or purpose for learning.

Cummins (1986, 1989) contrasts two general orientations to teaching: the transmission model and the reciprocal interaction model. The transmission model, Cummins argues, abets the disempowerment of poor students of color.

> The teacher's task is to impart knowledge or skills that he or she possesses to students who do not yet have these skills . . . . The teacher initiates and controls the interaction, constantly orienting it toward the achievement of instructional objectives. The curriculum . . . frequently focuses on the internal structure of the language or subject matter. Consequently, it focuses predominately on surface features of language or literacy. . . and emphasizes correct recall of content taught by means of highly structured drills and workbook exercises (Cummins 1986, p. 28).

In contrast, Cummins describes the reciprocal interaction model, which supports the empowerment of ethnic and language minority students and their academic success. Teachers guide and facilitate instruction rather than attempt to maintain absolute control of student learning; a more genuine dialogue takes place between teachers and students. "A central tenet of the reciprocal interaction model is that talking and writing are a means to learning" (Cummins 1986, p. 28). This orientation encourages collaborative learning and interaction among students and between students and teachers. Students tend to see academic tasks as relevant to their lives (Garcia 1991). Also, according to Cummins (1986), "This model emphasizes the development of higher level cognitive skills rather than just factual recall, and meaningful language use by students rather than the correction of surface forms" (p. 28). Often, in this approach, instruction in basic skills and academic content is organized around themes that students and teachers select together (Garcia 1991).

The reciprocal interaction model builds ethnic and language minority students' academic success through a variety of teaching methods and curricular programs. Teachers need a wide variety of teaching practices and strategies at hand to be able to respond appropriately to student needs (Anderson 1987, Nieto 1992). Although researchers have attempted to identify classroom practices that have successfully promoted learning among ethnic and language minority students (Natriello, McDill, and Pallas 1990; Slavin and Madden

1989), their work also raises important questions about the efficacy of some allegedly successful practices. For example, Reyes (1992) argues that currently popular forms of "process instruction" are not always successful with language minority students unless teachers make culturally and linguistically supportive adaptations.

> Teachers must rise above the euphoria over whole language and writing process and recognize that these programs are not perfect or equally successful for all. They are successful only to the extent that teachers understand the theories, assume the role of mediators, not merely facilitators, and create culturally and linguistically sensitive learning environments for all learners (Reyes 1992, p. 440).

The literature also agrees about the need for teachers to have a deep understanding of the subjects they teach so that they can create "the multiple representations necessary to address the diversity of prior experiences and understandings present in their classrooms" (McDiarmid 1989, p. 92).

Other strategies that teachers can employ to teach all students to high academic standards include modifying or developing curriculum materials to represent the perspectives and practices of different cultural groups (Sleeter and Grant 1988) and creating collaborative classroom environments through such practices as cooperative grouping, peer tutoring, and mixed-ability grouping (Garcia 1991, Hixson 1991, Quality Education for Minorities Project 1990). There is almost universal condemnation of ability grouping in elementary schools and tracking in secondary schools and a strong feeling that teachers need to be aware of the ways in which schools use these practices to structure inequality (Hodge 1990).

A final strategy for teachers that has substantial instructional benefits is to involve parents and other community members in authentic ways in the school program (Ada 1986, Grant 1991). Parents and other community members can play a significant role in determining what is an appropriate education for their children and youth (Delgado-Gaitan 1991, Zeichner 1991). According to Comer (1988), when adults across racial, class, and cultural lines share information and power within a school, students are more likely to be able to cross these lines and perform well in both languages and cultures.

Harrison (1993) argues that these interactions must be culturally appropriate in order for trust to develop between the school and the community. Harrison also contends that genuine parent and community empowerment is a more significant influence on school success than are particular instructional approaches.

Figure 4.1 summarizes this discussion of what teachers need to be like, to know, and to be able to do to teach all students to high academic standards.

FIGURE 4.1
A Pedagogy for Narrowing the Achievement Gap
In Urban Schools

Teachers have a clear sense of their own ethnic and cultural identities.

Teachers communicate high expectations to all students, along with the belief that all students can succeed.

Teachers are personally committed to achieving equity for all students, and they believe that they are capable of making a difference in students' learning.

Teachers develop a personal bond with their students and cease seeing them as "the other."

Teachers provide an academically challenging curriculum that includes attention to the development of higher-level cognitive skills.

Teachers focus instruction, guiding students to create meaning about content in an interactive, collaborative learning environment.

Teachers provide learning tasks that students see as meaningful.

Teachers provide a curriculum that includes the contributions and perspectives of the different ethnocultural groups that make up the society.

Teachers provide scaffolding that links the academically challenging and inclusive curriculum to cultural resources that students bring to school.

Teachers explicitly teach students the culture of the school **and** seek to maintain students' sense of ethnocultural pride and identity.

Teachers encourage parents and community members to become involved in students' education. Parents and community members are given a significant voice in making important school decisions related to programs, such as resources and staffing.

THE INADEQUACY OF CLASSROOM-BASED SOLUTIONS TO NARROWING THE ACHIEVEMENT GAP

Having high expectations for students, cultural congruence in instruction, culturally inclusive curriculum, knowledgeable teachers, and appropriate instructional strategies all contribute to narrowing the achievement gap in urban schools. By themselves, however, they are still not enough to overcome the effects of racism, language discrimination, social stratification, unequal resource distribution, and a history of discrimination against poor people of color (Carter and Goodwin 1994, Villegas 1988). As Weiner (1989) points out, while teacher education programs can turn out teachers who can instruct students in their classrooms with respect, creativity, and skill, they are no substitute for larger political and social movements that effectively alter systemic deficiencies in school systems and in society.

Granted, there are examples of schools where poor students of color achieve at high levels (National Coalition of Advocates for Students 1991). However, most urban teachers do not work in conditions where they can engage in the kind of complex and demanding teaching that makes high achievement possible (Weiner 1993). Changes in the ways in which teachers interact with students in classrooms must be accompanied or preceded by changes in schools' systemic and structural conditions. Otherwise, the highly interactive and demanding teaching that this chapter advocates will not become a reality except in a few exceptional schools. The kinds of changes that schools need include equalizing spending between rich and poor schools (Rotberg, Harvey, and Warner 1993), restructuring teachers' professional development to place an increased value on teacher learning (Lieberman 1989), and eliminating bureaucratic regulations that interfere with teachers' main academic mission.

THE TASK OF TEACHER EDUCATION

Teacher education is often overlooked in proposals to narrow the achievement gap in urban schools. Proposals for urban school reform often imply that if only we could identify the teaching and curriculum practices that lead to high achievement for all students, then all we would need do is "train" teachers to use these practices. This training model of teacher development dominates teacher education in urban schools. However, it is incompatible with the ambitious vision of teaching and schooling that is necessary to narrow the achievement gap (Little 1993).

The evidence on teacher learning makes clear that little will be accomplished if we put strategies such as cooperative learning and multicultural curriculum materials into the hands of culturally encapsulated and largely white, monolingual teachers and prospective teachers unless we change the ways they view themselves as cultural beings and poor students of color. Teacher education initiatives need to work at transforming some of the assumptions and attitudes teachers bring to teacher education. Nieto (1992) points out that the most important part of becoming a multicultural teacher is becoming a multicultural person. Teachers, like their students, interpret and give meaning to instruction through the concepts, categories, and world views they bring to learning (Wubbels 1992).

Developing teaching skills is only part of the job. Teacher education institutions also need to affect the kinds of people who go into urban schools to teach. Research identifies three dimensions to the task of preparing teachers for culturally diverse classrooms (Zeichner 1993). First, teacher education programs are limited in their ability to overcome the negative attitudes and low expectations that many prospective and current teachers hold for students of color and their families (Zeichner and Gore 1990). Therefore, teacher education programs need mechanisms that admit only people who have a commitment to teaching all students to high academic standards.

Currently, grade point averages, test scores, and the glowing testimony of young college students who want to be teachers because they "love kids" dominate admission practices in teacher education programs. But options exist. One is to use alternative route programs or programs with nontraditional structures, which tend to attract more diverse and mature prospective teachers than traditional university-based programs. Another is to employ selection procedures such as Haberman's (1987) interviews, which attempt to screen people especially for their potential to teach in urban schools.

A second dimension to educating teachers for diverse classrooms involves developing teachers' cultural sensitivity and intercultural teaching competence. Research shows that practices such as giving prospective teachers community field experiences and using noncertified community members as teacher educators, under particular conditions (e.g., clear guidelines, opportunities for reflection), contribute to teachers' ability to engage in culturally congruent instruction (Melnick and Zeichner 1994, Zeichner 1995, Zeichner and Hoeft 1996). These experiences range from very brief experiences and guided reflection activities associated with particular courses (e.g., Tran, Young, and DiLella 1994) to full-scale community immersion experiences where prospective teachers live and teach over an extended period of time in a culturally different community.

For example, The American Indian Reservation Project of Indiana University's School of Education provides a semester-long student-teaching experience in Native American schools and communities in the Southwest United States. (Mahan, Fortney, and Garcia 1983). During this semester, student teachers live in Native American communities and engage in substantial community field experiences in addition to their work in the schools. Paid part-time consultants from the communities assist in providing an intensive orientation for the immersion experience and support student teachers throughout the semester.

Several other teacher education programs such as the University of Wisconsin-Madison, the University of Houston, and New College in San Francisco also have attempted to develop stronger community links in initial teacher education with the goal of better preparing teachers to be successful with all students (McCaleb 1995, Zeichner and Melnick 1995). Evidence is accumulating that these community linkages result in many positive benefits with regard to preparing teachers for cultural diversity.

However, just as classroom solutions are inadequate without changes in the institutional context of teachers' work, socializing teachers within teacher education programs is inadequate without changes in the institutional environment in which such programs operate. The institutional context of teacher education programs is the third dimension of preparing teachers for cultural diversity. Many colleges and universities lack institutional commitment to diversity (Grant 1993). This, in turn, insulates faculty (Howey and Zimpher 1990). Together, these findings raise serious questions about the current capacity of teacher education institutions to support and sustain programs that prepare teachers for urban schools.

Fortunately, research identifies several promising strategies for strengthening the capacity of teacher education institutions. One strategy that is gaining particular favor is establishing consortiums that provide faculty expertise in multicultural education and staff development for teacher educators (Melnick and Zeichner 1994, Zeichner and Hoeft 1996). For example, the Associated Colleges of the Midwest Urban Education Program provides a semester of student teaching and community experiences in the city of Chicago along with several courses in multicultural and bilingual education for students from 14 liberal arts colleges (Zeichner and Melnick 1995). Several faculty members with successful urban teaching experience and an intimate knowledge of the various ethnic communities in Chicago provide an important component for those 14 colleges that is beyond the capacity of the institutions to provide themselves because of their locations and because of the experience of their faculties.

The research literature contains a growing consensus about what teachers need to be like, to know, and to be able to do to teach all students to high academic standards. This vision rests on teachers believing that all students can learn and taking responsibility for this task regardless of students' economic circumstances or skin color. The kinds of classrooms that will narrow the achievement gap in urban schools are highly interactive and collaborative. They are places where teachers let students know that they care about and hold high expectations for them. Instruction in these classrooms builds upon and respects the cultural resources and traditions that students bring to school. It integrates a variety of cultural perspectives, often around thematic units. At the same time, it inducts students into the culture of the school. The schools in which these classrooms exist value and support teacher learning and minimize bureaucratic conditions that distract teachers from their main academic mission with students.

Constance Clayton, former superintendent of the Philadelphia Public Schools, maintains that we do not need more research to tell us what we need to do to narrow the achievement gap in urban schools. The question is less the discovery of a new pedagogy through research than it is the emergence of a new politics. Clayton (1989), reiterating the position of the late Ronald Edmonds, contends that we already know how to teach all children successfully. The real issue is whether we as a society are serious about creating schools in which this pedagogical agenda can flourish. Similarly, we need to create the kinds of teacher education programs and professional development opportunities that can build this ambitious vision of schooling.

Ultimately, because of the impossibility of creating equal schools in an unequal society, narrowing the achievement gap between poor students of color in urban schools and their middle class peers depends on establishing the social preconditions necessary for school reform. This means dealing with massive inequities in society as a whole. Culturally relevant curriculum and instruction are only one small part of a society that provides all children access to decent and rewarding lives.

ENDNOTE

While this chapter has focused on the relations between white teachers and poor students of color, it cannot be assumed that teachers of color can necessarily translate their cultural knowledge into culturally relevant teaching practices (Montecinos 1995). Concerns about cultural and intercultural teaching competence are important issues for all teachers in all schools.

REFERENCES

Ada, A.F. (1986). "Creative Education for Bilingual Teachers." *Harvard Educational Review* 56, 4: 386-393.

Anderson, A. (1987). "Cultural Patterns Affecting Teacher and Student Expectations." In *Round Table Report: The Challenge —Preparing Teachers for Diverse Student Populations,* edited by R. Dash. Northridge, Calif.: Southern Service Center, Far West Laboratory for Educational Research and Development.

Au, K., and A. Kawakami. (1994). "Cultural Congruence in Instruction." In *Teaching Diverse Populations,* edited by E. Hollins, J. King, and W. Hayman. Albany, N.Y.: SUNY.

Banks, J. (1991). "Teaching Multicultural Literacy to Teachers." *Teaching Education* 4, 1: 135-144.

Bloch, M., and B.R. Tabachnick. (1991). *Learning Out of School: Critical Perspectives on the Theory of Cultural Compatibility*. Paper presented at the annual meeting of the American Educational Research Association, Chicago, Ill.

Bowers, C.A., and D. Flinders. (1990). *Responsive Teaching: An Ecological Approach to Classroom Patterns of Language, Culture, and Thought*. New York: Teachers College.

Carter, R.T., and A.L. Goodwin. (1994). "Racial Identity and Education." In *Review of Research in Education, 20*, edited by L. Darling-Hammond. Washington, D.C.: American Educational Research Association.

Cazden, C., and H. Mehan. (1990). "Principles from Sociology and Anthropology: Context, Code, Classroom, and Culture." In *Knowledge Base for the Beginning Teacher*, edited by M. Reynolds. Washington, D.C.: American Association of Colleges for Teacher Education.

Clayton, C. (1989). "Children of Value: We 'Can' Educate All Our Children." *The Nation* 249, 4: 132-135.

Coballes-Vega, C. (1992). "Considerations in Teaching of Culturally Diverse Children." *ERIC Digest*. ERIC Clearinghouse on Teacher-Education: Washington, D.C.

Cole, M., and P. Griffin. (1987). *Contextual Factors in Education*. Madison, Wisc.: Wisconsin Center for Education Research.

Comer, J. (1988). "Educating Poor Minority Children." *Scientific American* 259, 5: 42-48.

Cummins, J. (1986). "Empowering Minority Students: A Framework for Interventions." *Harvard Educational Review* 56, 1: 18, 36.

Cummins, J. (1989). *Empowering Minority Students*. Sacramento, Calif.: California Association for Bilingual Education.

Delgado-Gaitan, C. (1991). "Involving Parents in the Schools: A Process of Empowerment." *American Journal of Education* 100, 1: 20-46.

Delpit, L. (1986). "Skills and Other Dilemmas of a Progressive Black Educator." *Harvard Educational Review* 56, 4: 379-385.

Delpit, L. (1988). "The Silenced Dialogue: Power and Pedagogy in Educating Other People's Children." *Harvard Educational Review* 58, 3: 280-298.

Garcia, E. (1991). *Education of Linguistically and Culturally Diverse Students: Effective Instructional Practices*. Santa Cruz, Calif.: National Center for Research on Cultural Diversity and Second Language Learning.

Garcia, E. (1993). "Language, Culture, and Education." In *Review of Re-

search in Education, 19, edited by L. Darling-Hammond. Washington, D.C.: American Educational Research Association.

Goodlad, J. (1990). *Teachers for Our Nation's Schools.* San Francisco, Calif: Jossey-Bass.

Grant, C. (1991). "Educational Research and Teacher Training for Successfully Teaching Limited English Proficient Students." Paper presented at the Second National Research Symposium, Washington, D.C.

Grant, C. (1993). "The Multicultural Preparation of U.S. Teachers: Some Hard Truths." In *Inequality and Teacher Education,* edited by G. Verma. London: Falmer.

Haberman, M. (1987). *Recruiting and Selecting Teachers for Urban Schools.* New York: ERIC Clearinghouse on Urban Education, Institute for Urban and Minority Education.

Harrison, B. (1993). "Building Our House from the Rubbish Tree: Minority Directed Education." In *Minority Education: Anthropological Perspectives,* edited by E. Jacobs and C. Jordan. Norwood, N.J.: Ablex.

Heath, S.B. (1983). *Ways with Words: Language, Life and Work in Communities and Classrooms.* New York: Cambridge University.

Hixson, J. (1991). "Multicultural Issues in Teacher Education: Meeting the Challenge of Student Diversity." Paper presented at the annual meeting of the American Educational Research Association, Chicago, Ill.

Hodge, C. (1990). "Educators for a Truly Democratic System of Schooling." In *Access to Knowledge: An Agenda for Our Nation's Schools,* edited by J. Goodlad and P. Keating. New York: College Entrance Examination Board.

Hollins, E. (1982). "The Marva Collins Story Revisited: Implications for Regular Classroom Instruction." *Journal of Teacher Education* 33, 1: 37-40.

Hollins, E. (1990). "Debunking the Myth of a Monolithic White American Culture; or Moving Toward Cultural Inclusion." *American Behavioral Scientist* 34, 2: 201-209.

Hollins, E., and K. Spencer. (1990). "Restructuring Schools for Cultural Inclusion: Changing the Schooling Process for African-American Youngsters." *Journal of Education* 172, 2: 89-100.

Howey, K., and N. Zimpher. (1990). "Professors and Deans of Education." In *Handbook of Research on Teacher Education,* edited by W.R. Houston. New York: Macmillan.

Irvine, J.J. (1989). "Cultural Responsiveness in Teacher Education: Strategies to Prepare Majority Teachers for Successful Instruction of

Minority Students." Paper presented at the annual meeting of Project 30, Monterey, Calif.

Knapp, M.S., and P.M. Shields. (1990). "Reconceiving Academic Instruction for Children of Poverty." *Phi Delta Kappan* 71, 10: 752-758.

Knapp, M., and B. Turnbull. (1991). "Alternatives to Conventional Wisdom." In *Better Schools for the Children in Poverty: Alterations to Conventional Wisdom*, edited by M. Knapp and P. Shields. Berkeley, Calif.: McCutchan.

Ladson-Billings, G. (1990). "Cuturally Relevant Teaching." *The College Board Review* 155: 20-25.

Law, S.G., and D.S. Lane. (1987). "Multicultural Acceptance by Teacher Education Students." *Journal of Instructional Psychology* 14, 1: 3-9.

Leighton, M., A. Hightower, K. Wingley, E. Pechman, and H. McCollum. (1994). "Developing an Effective Instructional Workforce for Students with Limited English Proficiency." Paper presented at the annual meeting of the American Educational Research Association, New Orleans, La.

Lieberman, A. (1989). *Building a Professional Culture in Schools*. New York: Teachers College.

Little, J.W. (1993). "Teachers' Professional Development in a Climate of Educational Reform." *Educational Evaluation and Policy Analysis* 15, 2: 129-151.

Lucas, T., R. Henze, and R. Donato. (1990). "Promoting the Success of Latino Language-Minority Students: An Exploratory Study of Six High Schools." *Harvard Educational Review* 60, 3: 315-340.

Mahan, J., M. Fortney, and J. Garcia. (1983). "Linking the Community to Teacher Education: Toward a More Analytical Approach." *Action in Teacher Education* 5, 1-2: 1-10.

McCaleb, S.P. (1995). "Teaching: The Challenge of Change; Reclaiming Democracy Through Schooling." *Multicultural Education* 2, 3: 16-23.

McDiarmid, G.W. (1989). "What Do Prospective Teachers Learn in Their Liberal Arts Courses?" Issue paper 89-8. East Lansing, Mich.: National Center for Research on Teacher Learning.

McDiarmid, G.W., and J. Price. (1990). *Prospective Teachers' Views of Diverse Learners: A Study of the Participants in the ABCD Project*. East Lansing, Mich.: National Center for Research on Teacher Learning.

Mehan, H., and T. Trujillo. (1989). *Teacher Education Issues*. Research and Policy Series No. 4. Santa Barbara, Calif.: University of California, Linguistic Minority Research Project.

Melnick, S., and K. Zeichner. (1994). "Teacher Education for Cultural Diversity: Enhancing the Capacity of Teacher Education Institutions to Address Diversity Issues." Paper presented at the annual meeting of the American Association of Colleges for Teacher Education, Chicago, Ill.

Moll, L. (1988). "Some Key Issues in Teaching Latino Students." *Language Arts* 65, 5: 465-472.

Moll, L. (1992). "Literacy Research in Community and Classrooms: A Sociocultural Approach." In *Multidisciplinary Perspectives on Literacy Research*, edited by R. Beach, J.L. Green, M.L. Kamil, and T. Shanalas. Urbana, Ill.: National Council of Teachers of English.

Moll, L., C. Amanti, D. Neff, and N. Gonzalez. (1992). "Funds of Knowledge for Teaching: Using a Qualitative Approach to Connect Homes and Classrooms." *Theory into Practice* 31, 2: 132-141.

Moll, L., and R. Diaz. (1987). "Teaching Writing as Communication: The Use of Ethnographic Findings in Classroom Practice." In *Literacy and Schooling*, edited by D. Bloome. Norwood, N.J.: Ablex.

Moll, L., and J. Greenberg. (1990). "Creating Zones of Possibilities: Combining Social Context for Instruction." In *Vygotsky and Education: Instructional Implications and Applications of Sociohistorical Psychology*, edited by L. Moll. Cambridge, N.Y.: Cambridge University Press.

Montecinos, C. (1995). "Multicultural Teacher Education for a Culturally Diverse Teaching Force." In *Practicing What We Preach: Confronting Diversity in Teacher Education*, edited by R. Martin. Albany, N.Y.: SUNY Press.

National Coalition of Advocates for Students. (1991). *The Good Common School: Making the Vision Work for All Students.* Boston, Mass.: Author.

Natriello, G., E. McDill, and A. Pallas. (1990). *Schooling Disadvantaged Children: Racing Against Catastrophe.* New York: Teachers College.

Nieto, S. (1992). *Affirming Diversity: The Sociopolitical Context of Multicultural Education.* New York: Longman.

Oakes, J. (1985). *Keeping Track: How Schools Structure Inequality.* New Haven, Conn.: Yale University.

Olsen, L. and N. Mullen. (1990). *Embracing Diversity: Teachers' Voices from California's Classrooms.* San Francisco, Calif.: California Tomorrow Project.

Paine, L. (1989). "Orientation Towards Diversity: What Do Prospective Teachers Bring?" Research Report 89-9. East Lansing, Mich.: National Center for Research on Teacher Learning.

Quality Education for Minorities Project. (1990). *Education That Works: An Action Plan for the Education of Minorities*. Cambridge, Mass.: Author.

Reyes, M. (1992). "Challenging Venerable Assumptions: Literacy Instruction for Linguistically Different Students." *Harvard Educational Review* 62, 4: 427-446.

Rotberg, I., J.J. Harvey, and K. Warner. (1993). *Federal Policy Options for Improving the Education of Low Income Students*. Washington, D.C.: Rand Corporation.

Singer, E. (1988). "What Is Cultural Congruence and Why Are They Saying Such Terrible Things About It?" Occasional Paper No. 120. East Lansing, Mich.: Michigan State University, Institute for Research on Teaching.

Slavin, R., and N. Madden. (1989). "What Works for Students at Risk." *Educational Leadership* 46, 5: 4-13.

Sleeter, C., and C. Grant. (1988). *Making Choices for Multicultural Education*. Columbus, Ohio: Merrill.

Strickland, D., and C. Ascher. (1992). "Low Income African-American Children and Public Schooling." In *Handbook of Research on Curriculum*, edited by P. Jackson. Washington, D.C.: American Educational Research Association.

Tharp, R., and R. Gallimore. (1988). *Rousing Minds to Life: Teaching Learning and Schooling in Social Context*. New York: Cambridge University.

Tran, M.T., R. Young, and J. DiLella. (1994). "Multicultural Education Courses and the Student Teacher: Eliminating Stereotypical Attitudes in Our Ethnically Diverse Classrooms." *Journal of Teacher Education* 45, 3: 183-189.

Trueba, H. (1989). *Raising Silent Voices: Educating the Linguistic Minorities for the 21st Century*. New York: Newbury.

Villegas, A.M. (1988). "School Failures and Cultural Mismatch: Another View." *The Urban Review* 20, 4: 253-265.

Villegas, A.M. (1991). *Culturally Responsive Pedagogy for the 1990s and Beyond*. Princeton, N.J.: Educational Testing Service.

Villegas, A.M. (1993). "Restructuring Teacher Education for Diversity: The Innovative Curriculum." Paper presented at the annual meeting of the American Educational Research Association, Atlanta, Ga.

Watson, D., Z. Northcutt, and L. Rydell. (1989). "Teaching Bilingual Students Successfully." *Educational Leadership* 46, 5: 59-61.

Weiner, L. (1989). "Asking the Right Questions: An Analytic Framework for Reform of Urban Teacher Education." *The Urban Review* 21, 3: 151-161.

Weiner, L. (1993). *Preparing Teachers for Urban Schools.* New York: Teachers College.

Winfield, L. (1986). "Teacher Beliefs Toward At-Risk Students in Inner Urban Schools." *The Urban Review* 18, 4: 253-267.

Wubbels, T. (1992). "Taking Account of Student Teachers' Preconceptions." *Teaching and Teacher Education* 8, 2: 137, 150.

Zeichner, K. (1991). "Contradictions and Tensions in the Professionalization of Teaching and the Democratization of Schools." *Teachers College Record* 92, 3: 363-379.

Zeichner, K. (1993). "Educating Teachers for Cultural Diversity." Special report. East Lansing, Mich.: National Center for Research on Teacher Learning.

Zeichner, K. (1995). "Preparing Teachers for Cross-Cultural Teaching." In *Toward a Common Destiny: Race and Ethnic Relations in American Schools,* edited by W. Hawley and A. Jackson. San Francisco, Calif.: Jossey-Bass.

Zeichner, K., and J. Gore. (1990). "Teacher Socialization." In *Handbook of Research on Teacher Education,* edited by W.R. Houston. New York: Macmillan.

Zeichner, K., and K. Hoeft. (1996). "Teacher Socialization for Cultural Diversity." In *Handbook of Research on Teacher Education,* 2nd ed., edited by J. Sikula. New York: Macmillan.

Zeichner, K., and S. Melnick. (1995). "The Role of Community Field Experiences in Preparing Teachers for Cultural Diversity." Paper presented at the annual meeting of the American Association of Colleges of Teacher Education, Chicago, Ill.

5

Closing the Achievement Gap: Opportunity to Learn, Standards, and Assessment

Floraline Ingram Stevens

Over and over again, data from the National Assessment of Educational Progress (NAEP) show a large gap in achievement between African American and Hispanic students on the one hand and white students on the other. White students at ages 9, 13, and 17 perform at a higher level in reading, writing, science, and mathematics than the same age groups of African American and Hispanic students. While it is true that African American and Hispanic students' scores improved over a 20-year period while white students' achievement remained stagnant, the gap is still unacceptably large (Mullis, Owens, and Phillips 1990).

The story is the same among college-bound students (Fairtest 1993). In 1993, Asian and white students' SAT scores in mathematics and verbal competencies were 20 or more points above the scores of

African American and Hispanic students. The 1993 ACT scores
showed similar results: higher scores for Asian and white students.

The low academic achievement of African American students is a
national crisis. Just as we are coming into a technological and infor-
mation-based era that requires more skilled and talented individuals
to emerge from our schools, we are writing off a significantly large
portion of the U.S. population as unemployable and designating
them as permanent welfare recipients.

Often, educators, researchers, and policymakers attribute students' lack of academic achievement to the environment outside of
school—to "society's" negative impact on minority and poor students. And, to be sure, social and economic ills, cultural dissonance,
poor health, and counterproductive attitudes toward racial and ethnic diversity are well-documented deterrents to academic achievement (Stevens 1993a). But this achievement gap does not have to be.
Observers who attribute minority students' low achievement solely
to society's ills tend to dismiss the very important influences of
schools and teachers on student learning.

Opportunity to learn is a key factor in children's learning—perhaps the most critical one. In the United States, middle- and upper-
class parents have resources at their disposal to make up for any
deficiencies that might exist in school. That is not always the case
with families who are poor, non-English speaking, or living in
crowded or substandard housing. These parents may be unable to
provide their children with supportive, literate, and learning environments that supplement and enrich school instruction (Adams 1990).
That makes the opportunities to learn that schools provide poor and
minority students, or any other students from inadequate backgrounds, of paramount importance.

Originally, the concept of opportunity to learn (OTL) focused on
specific conditions of teaching and learning that generate high academic achievement. The emphasis was on what teachers do in their
classrooms when they teach students and whether or not they grant
students sufficient access to information and resources to enable
them to learn the curriculum for their age and grade. This chapter ex-
pands that narrow definition of opportunity to learn and presents an
OTL framework that encompasses not only standards for instructional quality but also for school and family support structures. In ad-

dition, it addresses standards of student performance and behavior, along with assessment, as critical components of opportunity to learn.

THE ORIGINAL OPPORTUNITY TO LEARN FRAMEWORK

In reviewing national and international research information and surveying 91 research directors from public school districts on opportunity to learn, Stevens (1993a) identified four variables to explain differences in students' academic achievement. These variables were tied principally to the providers of instruction, teachers, and school principals—not to students. The variables are: content coverage, content exposure, content emphasis, and quality of instructional delivery. These variables provide powerful insight into issues of equity and accountability in schools.

CONTENT COVERAGE

Content coverage has to do with whether or not students cover the core curriculum for their grade level or a particular subject area. When applied to assessment, content refers to the match between the content of the curriculum that was taught and the content of the test. Was there adequate and timely instruction of specific content and skills before students' took a test? Research shows that in many instances when comparative test scores were used to judge student achievement, the items on the test did not match the curriculum that was taught (Leinhardt 1983, Leinhardt and Seewald 1981, Walker and Schaffarzick 1974). When a match in coursework existed, student performance was consistent with teachers' reports of the degree to which they covered a topic (Yoon, Burstein, Gold, Chen, and Kim 1990). This begs the question, then: Is it fair to label as low achievers students who are not given the opportunity to learn knowledge and skills on which they are being tested?

Teachers who want to make sure that content coverage is adequately addressed in their classrooms must have more than a superficial knowledge of the content to be taught. They must decide the essential concepts and skills to be covered for students to successfully complete the grade-level course or subject matter topic. For example, in the Ten Schools Program in Los Angeles, deciding the content teachers needed to cover was necessary if they were to be held accountable for student learning in reading/language arts and mathematics. And the learning objectives for the program did specify percentile gains in those subject areas.

The program's teachers decided to meet by grade level to review California's curriculum frameworks for reading/language arts and mathematics. After scanning the frameworks, the teachers realized that all of the information required to be taught for each framework could not be covered adequately in one year. Through discussion, negotiation, and finally consensus, the teachers arrived at the core curriculum of concepts and skills that they believed must be taught to all children in each grade level. In addition, the teachers agreed to a schedule of when the concepts and skills would be taught. This allowed for a complimentary assessment program with the agreement that only the content scheduled to be taught would be assessed. That is, content to be taught was aligned with the content to be assessed.

This planning for content coverage determined when the teachers would cover the content and monitored whether or not the content was being covered in each of the classrooms. The assessment used was interval testing—a short test of three to four items per concept or skill to determine mastery. At that time, the interval testing followed a multiple-choice mode; however, alternative assessments (e.g., portfolios, performance-based assessment) could be used to determine whether or not the content was being covered successfully in each classroom.

CONTENT EXPOSURE

Content exposure concerns the time allotted for students to learn subject matter and the depth of teaching. The more time students spend on instructional experiences, the more they learn (Wiley 1990, Brophy and Good 1986). Some researchers have investigated components of opportunity to learn such as time spent reviewing, practicing, or applying a particular concept or the depth of content covered with particular groups of students. In surveying 1st grade Title I teachers, for example, Winfield (1987) found that they emphasized word-attack skills more than comprehension skills. This practice was contrary to research showing that instruction in decoding should be accompanied by instruction in comprehension to foster an ability to read independently (Doyle 1983).

The level of students' exposure to subject matter content is dependent upon accessible time. In poorly managed classrooms, off-task activities and events consume much of the teaching time. Again, in the Ten Schools Program (Stevens 1993b), during a 10-day observation of 4th grade reading periods, the allotted time for reading was lost or reduced due to schoolwide activities such as spelling bees, earthquake drills, and painting murals; teacher absences; and decisions to shorten the time allotted for reading.

Content exposure can be increased when teachers and administrators make plans to maximize the time. This is done by making certain periods of the day sacrosanct for critical subjects. No interruptions are allowed during this period throughout the school, and teachers commit to teach specified amounts of time for certain subjects. Teachers also have to be efficient in their time management. Certain housekeeping tasks such as taking attendance and collecting homework are routinized so they are completed quickly. Freiberg (1993b) describes how assigning leadership roles in classrooms eliminates many of the discipline problems that consume teachers' time in classrooms.

CONTENT EMPHASIS

Content emphasis determines which topics within the curriculum receive prominent attention and which students receive instruction in low- or higher-order skills. Floden, Porter, Schmidt, Freeman, and Schwitle (1981) and Shavelson and Stern (1981) showed that teachers choose what to emphasize in their classrooms according to personal experience; personal proficiency in a topic; perception of certain topics as more important than others; professional experiences; past experiences having to remediate certain topics; and the influence of past professors, education courses, textbooks, and other authorities. Schmidt (1990) found that textbooks and materials prepared by other teachers, more than class syllabi, influenced teachers in deciding what content to teach. Teachers also select which skills to teach and which skills to emphasize with which groups of students.

In a case study of Spanish-speaking kindergarten and 1st grade students, Goldenberg and Gallimore (1991) demonstrated that when teachers' attitudes about demographics and the backgrounds of parents negatively influenced their beliefs about students' readiness to learn a grade-level curriculum, they reduced the level of schoolwork they gave to their students, even though evidence indicated that this was not necessary.

A commitment to the concept that "all children can learn" should influence teachers to use strategies that include all students in their classrooms. Teachers need to be exposed to research information about the effects of using cooperative learning strategies. In addition, they need to be trained to effectively integrate cooperative and group learning strategies in their teaching. Teachers who attempt new strategies must feel that they are not at risk for trying something new. In their research, McLaughlin and Talbert (1993) emphasized the importance of groups of teachers trying new strategies and approaches together if the teaching changes were to continue in the classrooms.

Quality of Instructional Delivery

Quality of instructional delivery reveals how teaching practices in the classroom, particularly the coherent presentation of lessons, affect students' academic achievement. Quality instruction occurs when teachers have cognitive command of the subject matter, structure new information for students logically, help them relate it to what they already know, monitor their performance, and provide corrective feedback during lessons (Brophy and Good 1986). Teachers also need to explain how different parts of a lesson relate to one another (Stevenson and Stigler 1992).

A recent examination of an urban school district's reading program illustrates the need to take the quality of instructional delivery into account in assessment (Alkin, Doby, and Lindheim 1990). In this study, student outcome data showed that a new program failed to increase students' reading scores. But this evaluation also included case studies, and these revealed that some teachers had difficulty using the new program's literature-based approach. This, in turn, marred the quality of instructional delivery, which then lowered students' reading scores.

Teachers need to avoid what Haberman (1991) describes as the pedagogy of poverty. He described 14 teaching activities. In contrast, Haberman (1991) tells us that good teaching occurs when students in classrooms are

- involved with issues they regard as vital concerns;
- helped to see major concepts, big ideas, and general principles and are not merely engaged in the pursuit of isolated facts;
- involved in real-life experiences;
- redoing, polishing, or perfecting their work; and
- involved in the technology of information access.

For teachers to be able to do these things, Darling-Hammond (1990) tells us that their education should require the following:

- *Cognitive psychology* so they understand how people learn.
- *Developmental psychology* so they understand when children are ready to learn particular things in particular ways.
- *Learning theory and pedagogy* so they teach in developmentally and cognitively appropriate ways.
- *Professional ethics* so they manage schools' competing agendas in ways that keep the best interests of students at the forefront of their actions.

On a simplistic level, teachers observed teaching reading to 4th grade students in the Ten Schools Program were expected to do the following: state the reading objective for the lesson, assign activities that supported the lesson's objective, and teach concepts/skills relevant to the stated objective during the reading lesson. Teachers have to examine whether or not the lesson to be taught is coherent, with a beginning, middle, and end.

Stevenson and Stigler (1992) reported that one of the reasons the quality of instructional delivery in elementary schools in Japan and Taiwan differs from the United States is the amount of time allowed for teachers' collaboration. Japanese and Taiwanese teachers are given time during the day to prepare lessons and to meet, discuss, and perfect their teaching strategies and lessons. Teachers in the United States need the same time allowances for the same collaborative activities.

EXPANDING THE OTL FRAMEWORK

Reducing the achievement gap requires the combined efforts of schools, families, and students themselves. We now expand the original opportunity to learn support variables to include family support, school environment, and student behavior.

FAMILY SUPPORT

Families are children's first and primary educators. Children from families that have educational support structures in place have more opportunities to learn than children from families where no such structures exist.

Plentiful research evidence suggests that socioeconomic status (SES) serves as an indicator of the family's support for schooling. Low-SES, for example, seems to have a negative impact on the educational expectations that parents have for their children. The National Education Longitudinal Study of 1988, known as NELS:88 (Horn and West 1992), reported that as the level of parents' own education rose, larger percentages of parents expected their children to go to higher levels in school. Low-SES parents had lower expectations for their children's attainment of higher education levels. Only 31 percent expected their children to graduate from college or to earn a higher degree while more than 55 percent of middle-SES and 86 percent of high-SES parents had those expectations for their children. At the precollege level, two-parent families in which one or neither parent had completed high school held lower education-level expectations for their children than parents who both had diplomas and college degrees. This study also found that students from low-SES families whose parents never discussed future education plans with them were much more likely to drop out of school between 8th and 10th grades than students whose parents regularly discussed such topics.

Stevenson and Stigler (1992) suggest strengthening family support structures to increase the education and subsequent academic achievement of students in the United States. They recommend that:

- children spend more time doing homework,
- parents help children do their homework, and
- children spend more time in academic pursuits.

According to Cutler (1990), however, just the opposite is happening. In the United States, parents are turning their children over to television. Younger children watch more television than older children, and poor children more than affluent children. Children increasingly choose which television programs they watch, and they watch them alone without any mediating influence or commentary from adults. For most children, television takes the place of reading books, playing outdoors, or participating in activities that draw more profoundly upon their own imaginations.

In an international study of reading achievement, 9- and 13-year-olds in the United States devoted a higher percentage of time to television viewing than did any of the other children in the study. In those countries with heavy television viewing, light viewers scored highly on reading assessments and heavy viewers scored poorly. In the countries studied, downward reading trends confirmed that heavy television viewing is not readily compatible with high reading achievement of 14-year-olds (Elley 1992).

What is more serious about the impact of too much television is that it isolates children from their families and the family's nurturing. Children end up learning about the world vicariously instead of through their own interactions—conversations, games, chores, or other shared learning opportunities (Kubey and Csikszentmihalyi 1990).

SCHOOL ENVIRONMENT

The school environment plays a major role in students' opportunity to learn. Above all, this environment must provide students with meaningful access to learning. For this reason, school delivery standards can play an important role in reducing the academic achievement gap. Opportunity to learn, when included as part of school delivery standards, addresses curriculum standards, assessment standards, and student performance standards.

The traditional approach to curriculum and instruction has done little to reduce the achievement gap between minority and other students. Practices such as uniform instruction, remediation, workbook and worksheet drills, skills teaching, and ability grouping have not produced the needed results. New standards and approaches for in-

struction and curriculum that are more advantageous for all students, and particularly minority students, are in the offing. Hodges (1991) identifies these new approaches:
- identifying individual students' modes for learning,
- building on strengths children bring to school (dismissing the notion that children are empty slates),
- dialogue and discussion,
- modeling and interactive guided practice,
- strategy teaching (cognition),
- scaffolding to guide students in completing complex tasks,
- heterogeneous grouping,
- cooperative and team learning activities, and
- peer tutoring.

Wang, Haertel, and Walberg (1993) conducted a meta-analysis of school reform programs developed to address the educational needs of "at-risk" students. They describe these programs as focusing in three areas: developing new attitudes, implementing curriculum innovations, and using new instructional strategies.

Developing new attitudes includes:
- recognizing that students have prior knowledge,
- building on strengths rather than remediation, and
- distinguishing between cultural differences and deficits.

Curriculum innovations covers:
- focusing on complex real-life problems,
- embedding basic skills instruction into problem solving, and
- adding new content to students' prior knowledge and cultural background.

New instructional strategies include:
- modeling powerful thinking strategies,
- scaffolding complex tasks,
- employing reciprocal teaching, and
- using a variety of instructional approaches.

STUDENT BEHAVIOR

It is unrealistic to think that all students will arrive at school motivated and eager to learn. They do not. But teachers can manage the school environment to encourage motivation in students. McCaslan and Good (1992) suggest that teachers develop authoritative management systems. Such systems help students become active, self-regulated learners who are engaged in problem solving and meaningful learning, not just passive obedience or unfocused freedom.

Managing classrooms in which students do not have high standards for behavior and performance can be extremely hard. Teachers need help learning how to manage such classrooms. Ideally, they should learn this during preservice training; however, if they did not, it is crucial that they acquire this skill in inservice training.

Academic Performance Standards. Students' behavior ranges from total passivity and lack of any motivation to learn to relentless and aggressive academic competitiveness. Neither extreme is desirable. According to the new understanding of productive learning, students need to cooperate and collaborate in learning and problem-solving tasks. Smith (1992) tells us that social interactions bring about the growth of learning. In other words, what we learn from the company we keep stays with us through life.

Teachers can model a positive attitude toward problem solving if students do not have one. Similarly, teachers can assign students tasks that involve cooperative learning, that have more than one right answer, that use their prior knowledge and experience, and that have real meaning in their lives. According to Pintrich and DeGroot (1990a, 1990b), these are the things that influence students to be motivated, to be engaged, to be active, and to persist at learning tasks. Learning tasks that are challenging, meaningful and authentic—activities that are relevant to life outside of school—can facilitate the adoption of meaningful learning goals for students (Ames 1992, Brophy 1983, Meece 1991). Classrooms that do not offer students the opportunity to work on authentic tasks decrease students' motivation to learn.

In studying an inservice project aimed at broadening teachers' repertoire of instructional strategies, Kulm (n.d.) found that when teachers used alternative approaches to assessment, they also changed their approaches to teaching. They used more strategies that promoted students' higher-order thinking. Classroom activities enhanced meaning and understanding, developed student autonomy and independence, and helped students learn problem-solving strategies. Students changed their attitudes toward learning.

Behavior Standards. Students come from a variety of social, cultural, and home environments. Consequently, there is no one solution to getting them to become responsible for their behavior—especially if they don't have the support systems that build positive attitudes, high self-esteem, and persistence in performing learning tasks. Teachers in today's classrooms lose an inordinate amount of instructional time trying to reduce disruptive and nonproductive behavior. Reciting standards for behavior is one thing; implementing them is quite another.

The concept of resilience prompted the development of a successful management program for teachers in Texas. Freiberg (1993a) and other researchers developed a school and instructional management program called Consistency Management in five Houston, Texas, elementary schools to reduce the disciplinary problems that deprived teachers and students of valuable instructional time. Resilience, as defined by Freiberg, is a multifaceted process in which individuals demonstrate the ability to draw the best from the environment in which they find themselves. An earlier definition of resilience by Benard (1991) defines it as the use of prevention strategies to build and strengthen protective factors in families, schools, and communities.

The management program focused on assigning students age and developmentally appropriate responsibilities. Through this process, students took leadership roles in the classrooms, hallways, lunchroom, and playground. This strategy gave all students (not just the teacher's favorites) the opportunity to carry out important organizational roles in their classrooms. In all five schools, evaluation results after the program's first year showed statistically significant student achievement gains on nationally standardized tests and on the state's criterion-referenced tests. The number of disciplinary referrals and suspensions dropped as well (Freiberg 1993b).

ASSESSING ACHIEVEMENT AND OPPORTUNITY TO LEARN

We expect students to learn to apply knowledge, strategies, and concepts from various disciplines (e.g., mathematics, science, reading, social studies) in both their school learning and in their lives outside of school. But to really know if students are academically competent in these areas, we need accurate assessment information. Only through information from ongoing assessments of student learning can teachers know the impact of their teaching activities (Stevens 1993b).

Assessment is closely related to instruction and achievement. Its purpose is to inform teachers about the effectiveness of their teaching and the differences in students' learning. To provide this information, assessments must be valid, reliable, and fair. It is important, therefore, that classroom teachers have the knowledge to choose appropriate modes of assessment and to use them competently.

Most teachers, however, know little about the variety of assessment strategies available to them. They know even less about how to apply and integrate assessment with the subject matter they teach. These are major problems that preservice and inservice teacher training programs need to address if we are going to close the achievement gap.

Most preservice and inservice programs provide teachers little or no training in appropriate student assessment strategies to use in the classroom. To further exacerbate their lack of knowledge, most teachers work in isolation. Schools allocate little time during the day for teachers to collaborate, discuss their problems, or share information about what they do know about assessment. Even if some teachers have "good" assessment information, it is difficult and sometimes impossible for them to share that information with others.

Research by McLaughlin and Talbert (1993) showed that teachers who remained isolated while attempting new strategies became frustrated and discouraged and could not sustain the strategies over time. Those teachers who were able to adapt to new practices belonged to an "active professional community" that encouraged them to transform their teaching practices. The result would probably be the same if the strategies had to do with testing and assessment; that is, if teachers were coping with the problem of how to assess and measure student progress accurately and how to transfer the results of the assessment to their teaching practices.

It is critical that teachers' knowledge of their craft include skill in assessment and testing. We are quick to attribute low test scores solely to the lack of students' own efforts or to their membership in poor or minority groups. Seldom do we attribute low scores to a teacher's performance in the classroom. We will not know the true effects of instructional practices on different groups of students until opportunity to learn becomes part of student outcome data.

For this to happen, teachers need to be trained to apply and integrate assessment strategies with the subject matter being taught, to collect the data, to analyze the information that the assessment produces, and to determine where to modify their teaching practices. Schools need to support teachers by providing time for staff to share, collaborate, and discuss the impact of their teaching and assessment practices. Similarly, preservice programs in college and university schools of education need to make the principles of opportunity to learn part of their own postsecondary education reform efforts.

APPROACHES TO MEASURING OTL

Opportunity to learn changes the way we look at student outcome data. Just as the international studies (principally those from the International Association for Evaluation of Educational Achievement) looked beyond race, SES, and gender to the instructional and cultural practices in different countries, we must do the same when looking at different groups of students in the United States. But opportunity to learn is still relatively unknown to most school districts. Moreover, ways to assess opportunity to learn are still in the development stage.

TEACHER LOGS

Porter (1993) recommended using teacher logs as one measure of opportunity to learn. He cited a study in which teachers measured several OTL indicators by recording information about time spent on content topics, amount of time and emphasis on different modes of instruction and student activities, and the portion of a class period spent on activities not directly related to the academic content of the course. A system of OTL indicators, according to Porter, can describe the kinds of educational opportunities schools provide, help chart the progress of schools, and explain student achievement.

OBSERVATIONS

Several researchers (Stevens 1993b; Stevenson and Stigler 1992; Dorr-Bremme, Keesling, and King 1984) demonstrated that structured classroom observations can measure opportunity to learn. For example, in a case study of 4th grade reading, observational data were collected and analyzed within the following dimensions of OTL:

• percentage of teaching periods within a specified number of days devoted to the subject content;

• percentage of time devoted to teaching subject content within a period; and

• amount of coherency in the lesson presented.

SURVEYS

Goertz (1994) reported that opportunity to learn can be measured through survey items, as several were in the 1990 NAEP Trial State Assessment. NAEP assessed the following OTL variables: students' access to calculators and computers, teachers' access to adequate instructional resources, and teachers' level of training. These variables were regressed against the state NAEP proficiency scores. However, the influence of student SES could not be factored out of the relationship.

INTERVAL TESTING AND SMALL ASSESSMENT TASKS

Stevens (1993a) reported that interval testing and assessment of small tasks focused upon particular skills or concepts can provide teachers with OTL information about the impact and quality of their instructional delivery. In a study of 10 elementary schools, teachers and their administrators used this OTL information to decide what type of staff development would improve their teaching practices.

The development and use of OTL indicators, standards, and assessments will help teachers and administrators obtain information to make meaningful decisions for improving teaching practices and classroom management, supporting and enhancing students' resilience, and creating enriched school environments. Both the home and the classroom must provide students with the opportunity to learn and support their resiliency in choosing positive behaviors. Closing the achievement gap, while complex, is not impossible. The key elements we need for success are collaboration and cooperation among families, schools, and students.

In addition, communication between families and schools can become a positive flow of information about how home activities can support and sustain students' academic achievement. When these collective efforts come together, systemic and productive change can occur and we can begin to close the achievement gap.

REFERENCES

Adams, M. (1990). *Beginning to Read: Thinking and Learning about Print.* Cambridge, Mass.: MIT.

Alkin, M., W. Doby, and E. Lindheim. (1990). *Ten Schools Program Reports Case Studies: 1988-89.* Los Angeles, Calif.: Los Angeles Unified School District.

Ames, C. (1992). "Classrooms: Goals, Structures, and Student Motivation." *Journal of Educational Psychology* 84, 3: 261-271.

Benard, B. (1991). *Fostering Resiliency in Kids: Protective Factors in Family, School and Community.* Portland, Ore.: Western Regional Center for Drug-Free Schools and Communities, Far West Laboratory for Educational Research and Development.

Brophy, J. (1983). "Conceptualizing Student Motivation." *Educational Psychologist* 18: 200-215.

Brophy, J., and T. Good. (1986). "Teacher Behavior and Student Achievement." In *Handbook of Research on Teaching,* edited by M. Wittrock. New York: MacMillan.

Cutler, B. (November 1990). "Where Does the Free Time Go?" *American Demographics,* 38.

Darling-Hammond, L. (1990). "Teacher Professionalism: Why and How?" In *Schools as Collaborative Cultures: Creating the Future Now,* edited by A. Lieberman. New York: Falcon Press.

Dorr-Bremme, D., W. Keesling, and N. King. (1984). *Research on Effective and Ineffective Classroom Practices in Chapter 2 Schools.* (Publication

450). Los Angeles, Calif: Los Angeles Unified School District, Research and Evaluation Branch.

Doyle, W. (1983). "Academic Work." *Review of Educational Research* 53, 2: 159-199.

Elley, W.B. (1992). *How in the World Do Students Read? The IEA Study of Reading Literacy.* Hamburg, Germany: The International Association for the Evaluation of Educational Achievement, IEA.

Fairtest. (1993). "Gender Gap Grows on SAT and ACT." *Fairtest Examiner* 7, 3: 1, 4.

Floden, R., A. Porter, W. Schmidt, D. Freeman, and J. Schwitle. (1981). "Responses to Curriculum Pressures: A Policy Capturing Study of Teacher Decisions about Context." *Journal of Educational Psychology* 73: 129-141.

Freiberg, J. (1993a). "Understanding Resilience: Implications for Inner-City Schools and Their Near and Far Communities." In *Educational Resilience in Inner-City America: Challenges and Prospects,* edited by M.C. Wang and E.W. Gordon. Hillsdale, N.J.: Lawrence Erlbaum.

Freiberg, J. (1993b). "A School that Fosters Resilience in Inner-City Youth." *The Journal of Negro Education* 62, 8: 364-376.

Goertz, M. (1994). *Opportunity to Learn: Instructional Practices in Eighth Grade Mathematics. Data from the 1990 NAEP Trial State Assessment, CPRE.* (Research Report No. 32). New Brunswick, N.J.: Rutgers, The State University of New Jersey.

Goldenberg, C., and R. Gallimore. (1991). "Local Knowledge, Research Knowledge, and Educational Change: A Case Study of Early Spanish Reading Improvement." *Educational Researcher* 20, 8: 2-14.

Haberman, M. (1991). "The Pedagogy of Poverty Versus Good Teaching." *Phi Delta Kappan* 73, 4: 290-294.

Hodges, H. (1991). "Reading: Standards for Curriculum and Instruction." A working outline prepared for the Association for Supervision and Curriculum Development, Alexandria, Va.

Horn, L., and J. West. (1992). *National Education Longitudinal Study of 1988: A Profile of Parents of Eighth Graders.* Washington, D.C.: National Center for Education Statistics.

Kubey, R., and M. Csikszentmihalyi. (1990). *Television and the Quality of Life: How Viewing Shapes Everyday Experience.* Hillsdale, N.J.: Lawrence Erlbaum.

Kulm, J. (n.d.). "A Study of the Effects of Alternative Assessment in Mathematics Classrooms." Unpublished manuscript.

Leinhardt, G. (1983). "Overlap: Testing Whether It Is Taught." In *The Courts, Validity, and Minimum Competency Testing*, edited by G.F. Madeus. Boston, Mass.: Kluweer-Nijhoff.

Leinhardt, G., and A. Seewald. (1981). "Overlap: What's Tested, What's Taught?" *Journal of Educational Measurement* 18, 2: 85-96.

McCaslan, M., and T. Good. (1992). "Compliant Cognition: The Misalliance of Management and Instructional Goals in Current School Reform." *Educational Researcher* 21, 3: 4-17.

McLaughlin, M., and J. Talbert. (1993). *Contexts that Matter for Teaching and Learning: Strategic Opportunities for Meeting the Nation's Educational Goals*. Stanford, Calif.: Center for Research on the Context of Secondary School Teaching, Stanford University.

Meece, J. (1991). "The Classroom Context and Children's Motivational Goals." In *Advances in Motivation and Achievement, Vol. 7*, edited by M. Maehr and P. Pintrich. Greenwich, Conn.: JAI.

Mullis, I., E. Owens, and G. Phillips. (1990). *America's Challenge: Accelerating Academic Achievement. A Summary of Findings from 20 Years of NAEP*. Princeton, N.J.: Educational Testing Service.

Pintrich, P., and E. DeGroot. (1990a). "Motivational and Self-Regulated Learning Components of Classroom Academic Performance." *Journal of Educational Psychology* 82,1: 33-40.

Pintrich, P., and E. DeGroot. (1990b). "Quantitative and Qualitative Perspectives on Student Motivational Beliefs and Self-Regulated Learning." Paper presented at the annual meeting of the American Educational Research Association, Boston, Mass.

Porter, A. (1993). *Opportunity to Learn*. (Brief No. 7). Madison, Wisc.: Center on Organization and Restructuring of Schools.

Schmidt, W. (1990). *The Distribution of Instructional Time to Mathematical Content: One Aspect of Opportunity to Learn*. East Lansing, Mich.: Michigan State University, National Center for Research on Teacher Education.

Shavelson, R., and P. Stern. (1981). "Research on Teachers' Pedagogical Thoughts, Judgments, Decisions, and Behaviors." *Review of Educational Research* 5, 4: 275-277.

Smith, F. (1992). "Learning to Read: The Never Ending Debate." *Phi Delta Kappan* 73, 6: 432-441.

Stevens, F. (1993a). *Opportunity to Learn: Issues of Equity for Poor and Minority Students*. Washington, D.C.: National Center for Education Statistics.

Stevens, F. (1993b). "Applying an Opportunity to Learn Conceptual Framework to the Investigation of the Effects of Teaching Practices Via Secondary Analysis of Multiple-Case Study Summary Data." *Journal of Negro Education* 62, 8: 232-248.

Stevenson, H., and J. Stigler. (1992). *The Learning Gap: Why Our Schools Are Failing and What We Can Learn from Japanese and Chinese Education.* New York: Summit Books.

Walker, D., and J. Schaffarzick. (1974). "Comparing Curricula." *Review of Educational Research* 44: 83-111.

Wang, M., G. Haertel, and H. Walberg. (1993). "Toward a Knowledge Base for School Learning." *Review of Educational Research* 63, 3: 249-294.

Wiley, D. (1990). *Opportunity to Learn: A Briefing for the Advisory Council on Education Statistics.* Washington, D.C.: National Center for Education Statistics.

Winfield, L. (1987). "Teachers' Estimates of Test Content Covered in Class and First-Grade Students' Reading Achievement." *Elementary School Journal* 87, 4: 438-445.

Yoon, B., L. Burstein, K. Gold, Z. Chen, and K. Kim. (1990). "Validating Teachers' Report of Content Coverage: An Example from Secondary School Mathematics." Paper presented at the annual meeting of the National Council on Measurement in Education, Boston, Mass.

6

Fostering Resiliency in Urban Schools

BONNIE BENARD

A recent cartoon provocatively sums up the context in which institutions that serve youth must function today. It shows a journalist typing the following headline: "All Schools To Be Called 'Prisons.' Public Supports Massive Funding. Ends Education Crisis."

Even after a decade of clarion calls about deteriorating conditions for U.S. children, child advocacy organizations such as the Children's Defense Fund report that the decline of healthy childhood continues steadily. Indicators show decreases in perinatal care, quality child care, parental employment, safe schools, and community support. Other indicators show steady increases in the number of youth living in poverty or in prisons; who are homeless, afflicted with AIDS, pregnant, addicted, affiliated with gangs, or perpetrators or victims of violence; or who have dropped out of school (Children's Defense Fund 1994).

Political scientist Barber (1993) states, "Clearly, the social contract that obliges adults to pay taxes so that children can be educated is in imminent danger of collapse. Yet for all the astonishing statistics, more astonishing still is that no one seems to be listening."

Barber continues, "As America's educational system crumbles, the pundits, instead of looking for solutions, search busily for scapegoats. Some assail the teachers—those 'Profscam' pedagogues trained in the licentious sixties who, as aging hippies, are supposedly still subverting the schools—for producing a dire illiteracy. Others turn on the kids themselves. At the same moment as we are transferring our responsibilities to the shoulders of the next generation, we are blaming them for our own generation's most conspicuous failures" (p. 40). As has become clear in California's recently passed crime bill and in the debate surrounding the federal crime bill, policymakers would rather spend billions of dollars to build prisons in which to lock kids up than thousands of dollars to send them to decent schools.

Making children, their families, and their schools scapegoats for society's negligence is not a universal phenomenon. It specifically targets those people who live in what researcher Polakow (1993) calls the "other" United States: the men, women, and children—usually of color—who inhabit poverty-stricken inner cities in the United States. Echoing Barber, Polakow (1993) states, "Out of this landscape of otherness we have constituted a discourse of concealment that fails to name the full face of poverty, that allows the horrors of public indifference to make possible a 'social asphyxia' described by Victor Hugo in 1862. . .as 'the ruin of women by starvation and the atrophy of childhood by physical and spiritual night'"(p. 2).

While reformers in western Europe heeded Victor Hugo and Charles Dickens and eradicated much of the poverty that beset single women and children, Polakow (1993) says that in the United States, "Poverty has been artfully reconfigured as a social/cultural/psychological pathology, corroborated by a public educational discourse of deficiency and remediation" (p. 3).

Increasingly, literature and practice in the fields of public health, mental health, and education focus on "at-risk" youth and families. More than 40 years of social science research clearly identifies poverty as the factor most likely to put an individual at risk of experiencing social problems such as drug abuse, teen pregnancy, child abuse, and violence. Nonetheless, we persist in "blaming the victim" not only for exhibiting the symptoms of poverty but also for the poverty itself (Currie 1993, Polakow 1993, Schor 1992, Wilson 1987).

This attitude has given rise to a "cultural deficit" model for educational policies and practices. As Polakow (1993) eloquently states, "It is otherness that is at risk, reframed as an individual or minority problem in need of redress. [This] renaming and the redefining of the worlds of those who are destitute permit public denial of our social responsibility for poor mothers and their children" (p. 3) and, as Barber (1993) says, for the schools that educate them.

This cultural deficit perspective focuses educational discourse on the problems of school failure, the "achievement gap," and dropout rates. Stevenson and Ellsworth (1993) explain, "A common perception among both educators and the public is that students [fail and] drop out of school because of personal deficiencies and/or family or cultural deprivation. Contributing to this perception is a research and policy agenda, as well as professional and popular literature on school dropouts that have concentrated on the personal and demographic characteristics of the dropouts themselves." The message, once again, is that students are the problem. This, in turn, "implies that schools bear little responsibility for students dropping out and therefore can take few actions to reduce the number of dropouts" (p. 259).

RESILIENCY RESEARCH

Despite such overwhelming perceptions, there have always been and there will always be educators who successfully educate children labeled "high risk." These educators concentrate on children's strengths, show compassion for their lives, believe the children—and their families—are doing the best they can given their circumstances, and welcome them "at the table" (Ashton-Warner 1963, Carini 1982, Heath 1983, Kidder 1990, Kohl 1967). Recently, though, a body of international, cross-cultural, lifespan developmental research has emerged around what these educators do. The research documents the powerful role that adults—be they teachers, principals, counselors, coaches, or janitors—play in fostering children's resiliency, that is, in encouraging children to successfully adapt despite risk and adversity (Maston 1994; Garmezy 1991; Hetherington, Cox, and Cox

1982; Kellam 1982; Wallerstein and Blakeslee 1990; Werner and Smith 1992). Moreover, it consistently finds that at least half—and often two-thirds—of children growing up in families where parents were mentally ill, alcoholic, abusive, or criminal, or in communities that were poverty stricken or torn by war, do become competent, healthy, and successful adults—*if* as children and youth they experienced nurturing somewhere in their lives (Rutter 1985, Werner and Smith 1992).

Benard (1991b) summarizes four traits commonly found in resilient individuals. These traits are social competence, problem-solving skills, autonomy, and a sense of purpose and future.

Social competence consists of relationship skills. It involves responsiveness, especially the ability to elicit positive responses from others; flexibility, including the ability to move back and forth between primary culture and dominant culture (cross-cultural competence); and empathy, caring, communication skills, and a sense of humor.

Problem-solving skills encompass the ability to plan; to be resourceful in seeking help from others; and to think critically, creatively, reflectively, and flexibly, trying out alternate solutions to both cognitive and social problems. Other critical components of problem solving are the development of a critical consciousness; an awareness of the structures of oppression (whether by an alcoholic parent, an insensitive school, or a racist society); and the creation of strategies for overcoming them.

Autonomy has to do with a sense of one's own identity. It involves an ability to act independently and to exert some control over one's environment, and it includes a sense of task mastery, internal locus of control, self-agency, and self-efficacy. The development of resistance (refusing to accept negative messages about oneself or one's culture) and of detachment (distancing oneself from parental, school, or community dysfunction) serves as a powerful protector of autonomy.

A sense of purpose and future signifies goal direction, educational aspirations, achievement motivation, persistence, hopefulness, optimism, and spiritual connectedness.

Resilience is not a genetic trait that only a few "superkids" possess, as some journalists and even several researchers would have us believe. Lifespan studies show that all human beings have the innate capacity and self-right to adapt to their circumstances (Lifton 1993). Such studies, Werner and Smith (1992) explain, "offer us a more optimistic outlook than the perspective that can be gleaned from the literature on the negative consequences of perinatal trauma, caregiving deficits, and chronic poverty. They provide us with a corrective lens— an awareness of the self-righting tendencies that move children toward normal adult development under all but the most persistent adverse circumstances" (p. 202).

The literature on inner-city school effectiveness (Edmonds 1986; Rutter, Maughan, Mortimore, Ouston, and Smith 1979) and the rich body of ethnographic studies in which youth, families, and teachers explain their success and failure corroborates the research on resiliency. These investigations produce a very clear picture of school structures, organizations, and relationships that help youth develop resilience and overcome the odds (Erickson 1987; Farrell 1990; Fine 1991; Gandara 1995; Heath and McLaughlin 1993; Institute for Education in Transformation 1992; Kagan 1990; Kozol 1991; Lefkowitz 1987; McLaughlin, Irby, and Langman 1994; Mehan, Hubbard, and Villanueva 1994; Phelan, Davidson, and Cao 1992; Polakow 1993; Wehlage, Rutter, Smith, Lesko, and Fernandez 1989; Weis and Fine 1993).

Research associates a clear pattern of characteristics with family, school, or community environments that foster resiliency in children. Called "protective factors," these characteristics appear to alter—or even reverse—potential negative outcomes and enable individuals to circumvent life stresses. Protective factors fall into three broad categories: caring and support, positive and high expectations, and opportunities for meaningful participation in school (Benard 1991b).

CARING AND SUPPORT

Given the incredible stresses in urban families and communities, the inner-city school is a refuge for many children. School serves as a "protective shield to help children withstand the multiple vicissitudes that they can expect of a stressful world" (Garmezy 1991, p. 427). Research by Garbarino, Dubrow, Kostelny, and Pardo (1992) on children growing up in "war zones" in the United States and elsewhere found that, "Despite the overwhelming pressures in the environment, 75-80 percent of the children can use school activities as a support for healthy adjustment and achievement when schools are sensitive to them and their burdens" (p. 121). Listen to Naomi, age 17: "School was my church, it was my religion. It was constant, the only thing that I could count on every day. . . . I would not be here if it was not for school" (Children's Express 1993).

Werner and Smith (1989) studied all the children born on the island of Kauai in 1955 and found that, "Among the most frequently encountered positive role models in the lives of [these] children, outside of the family circle, was a favorite teacher. For the resilient youngster a special teacher was not just an instructor for academic skills, but also a confidante and positive model for personal identification" (p. 162). Noddings's (1992) work on caring led her to believe that for schools to be true centers of learning, they must embrace caring in all its forms—care for self, for intimate others, for associates and acquaintances, for distant others, for nonhuman animals, for plants and the physical environment, for the human-made world of objects and instruments, and for ideas.

In an earlier article, Noddings writes that as traditional structures of caring deteriorate, schools must fill the void, giving teachers and students a place to talk together and share experiences. Commenting on the key to school success, not only for children labeled "at risk" but for all children, Noddings said: "My guess is that when schools focus on what really matters in life, the cognitive ends we now pursue so painfully and artificially will be achieved somewhat more naturally. . . . It is obvious that children will work harder and do things—even odd things like adding fractions—for people they love and trust" (Noddings 1988, p. 38).

The following story (based on a real study) illustrates what resiliency research has found: the power of a teacher to make a difference.

> A college professor had his sociology class go into the Baltimore slums to get case histories of 200 young boys. They were asked to write an evaluation of each boy's future. In every case the students wrote, "He hasn't got a chance." Twenty-five years later another sociology professor came across the earlier study. He had his students follow up on the project to see what had happened to these boys. With the ex-

ception of 20 boys who had moved away or died, the students learned that 176 of the remaining 180 had achieved more than ordinary success as lawyers, doctors and businessmen.

The professor was astounded and decided to pursue the matter further. Fortunately, all the men were in the area and he was able to ask each one, "How do you account for your success?" In each case the reply came with feeling, "There was a teacher."

The teacher was still alive, so he sought her out and asked the old but still alert lady what magic formula she had used to pull these boys out of the slums into successful achievement. The teacher's eyes sparkled and her lips broke into a gentle smile. "It's really very simple," she said. "I loved those boys" (Butterworth 1993, p. 3-4).

In longitudinal and ethnographic studies, youth of all ages, all colors, and all places tell us over and over again that what they want is a teacher who cares. Stanford University's Center for Research on the Context of Secondary School Teaching found in a study of adolescents that, "The number of student references to wanting caring teachers is so great that we believe it speaks to the quiet desperation and loneliness of many adolescents in today's society" (Phelan et al. 1992, p. 698). Furthermore, studies of school dropouts repeatedly identify the lack of anyone who cared about them as the main reason for these youth leaving school (Higgins 1988, Stevenson and Ellsworth 1993).

A recent study of young women who dropped out of school or who dropped out and reentered school, rated alternative programs and schools highly:

- "We get treated like adults."
- "Teachers and counselors pay a lot of attention to us."
- "We work in smaller groups."
- "We come here because we want to learn."
- "Students help each other out."
- "Students get to know each other better."
- "It's easy to have confidence here." (NOW Legal Defense and Education Fund 1988, p. 7)

Affiliation is a basic human need from which individuals draw support, a sense of belonging, and motivation. As personality theorist Erikson (1963) long ago pointed out, the first stage of development in any system requires the establishment of trust and the sense of safety, constancy, and predictability. Findings in brain research document that like resilience, intelligence is innate to all human beings, but—and again paralleling resilience—it unfolds in the presence of a nurturing environment. Pearce (1992), a major synthesizer and translator of this research, writes, "All the infant-child (and the adult as well) wants to do is what nature intended: learn, build those structures of knowledge. And all that is needed for this is an appropriate environment—being surrounded by a mature, intelligent intellect, open to mind's possibilities and tempered by heart's wisdom" (p. 14).

Caring in school is seeing possibilities in each child and using one's wisdom of the heart. This means that teachers and other personnel need to muster the compassion to look beyond the hostility in some youth to the insecurities that lie underneath. As Werner and Smith (1992) write, "The resilient youngsters in our study all had at least one person in their lives who accepted them unconditionally, regardless of temperamental idiosyncrasies, physical attractiveness, or intelligence" (p. 205). The power of caring is illustrated in the following account of a school bus driver:

> I recently visited a rather progressive school district in Arkansas. I had been asked to assist in the development of an evolving participatory effort, including a redefinition of the district purpose. As I was working in one of the schools, one of the teachers told me that her students were quite distressed because their bus driver was retiring. She had repeatedly tried to get her students to accept the driver's retirement, but felt she had failed. She asked me if I would talk to the children. I agreed and asked her to tell me all she knew about the bus driver.
>
> "I know his name is Mike," she told me, "and that he appears to be quite kind. However, he usually has trouble getting his bus loaded on time after school."
>
> My talk with the children was brief. All they could do was express their distress at losing Mike and they asked me to make him stay "cause he's our friend."

With only one thing left to do, I went looking for Mike, who turned out to be a very pleasant-looking man in his mid-sixties. I apologized for intruding into his business and assured him that I was not trying to dissuade him from retirement. "I am interested only in learning why the children, in your opinion, hold you in such high regard," I told him directly.

Mike said that about three years earlier he had overheard the principal tell the teachers that a corporate purpose had been adopted and described this purpose as the need to get the kids to believe in themselves and be proud of their accomplishments. Mike had been on the route for a long time and knew that most of his kids went home to an empty house. He also told me he noticed that the kids often left school papers on the bus, even the ones with stars and smiley faces. He concluded they had no one to share the papers with when they arrived home. Keeping the new purpose in mind, Mike began asking the students as they entered the bus to show him the papers that made them feel good.

"Do you think I did the right thing?" he asked me. "It does take longer to load the bus" (Golarz and Golarz 1995).

Teachers must "reach beyond the resistance," as educator Kohl (1994) advises, and connect with a youth's soul. Truly and carefully listening to a youth's story is a powerful signal that a teacher believes and accepts the youth and cares about him or her. In her research on resilient survivors of childhood abuse and trauma, psychologist Miller (1990) claims, "On closer examination [of a person's childhood,] it turns out in every case that a sympathetic and helpful witness confirmed the child's perceptions, thus making it possible for him to recognize that he had been wronged" (pp. 50-51).

While it is impossible to overemphasize the importance of teachers as caregivers, we must not overlook the role of caring peers and friends in the development of resiliency and school success (Kohn 1991). Werner and Smith's (1989) study found caring friends were a major factor in the development of resiliency among the children of Kauai. Extensive research by Johnson and Johnson (1990), as well as by Slavin (1990), on the positive social and academic outcomes of cooperative learning and group development repeatedly confirms the

importance of peer social support. Other studies of prevention programs that focus on increasing social support to youth demonstrate
significant positive outcomes such as reduced levels of alcohol and
drug use and dropping out of school (Felner, Aber, Primavera, and
Cauce 1985, Eggert and Herting 1991, Mehan et al. 1994). Similarly,
numerous programs in which peers help peers exponentially increase
the caregiving resources available to youth and attest to the power of
a caring ethic in school (Benard 1990a). The story of Alexandra illustrates the power of a caring ethic:

> I first moved away from my father the day before I started
> high school. As I headed toward my new home . . . I remem-
> bered the many times I had to cook and eat alone, waiting for
> my dad to remember me and come home. I knew I deserved
> better. Since that day, however, I have become too familiar
> with moving from household to household. . . . In the middle
> of my junior year, I found myself without a home, a steady
> source of income, or a family. . . . I almost lost my sense of
> identity and any motivation. . . . During these difficult times, I
> found the stability that was lacking in my personal life at
> school. I went to the Peer Resource Center . . . because I
> needed support. . . . I became very active in the Peer Resource
> Center, where I was able to form close ties while helping oth-
> ers with difficulties like mine. . . . Although I have had an
> overwhelmingly stressful past, my experiences have been es-
> sential in my growth as a person and as a friend. I am proud
> of the fact that my forced independence empowered me to
> find the initiative and strength to provide for my own well-
> being (Kent 1995).

Creating a schoolwide ethos or climate of caring means teachers,
too, must have caring support networks. McLaughlin's (1990) work
demonstrates that collegial support is not only the key to sustaining
change within a school but is also the critical variable leading to
higher student achievement (McLaughlin and Talbert 1993). The re-
peated success of Levin's (1988) Accelerated Schools and James
Comer's (1984) School Development Program is due, in part, to the
caring, supportive relationships these schools have with the families
of their students.

The caring ethic is obviously not a program or a strategy, per se,
but a way of being in the world. It is a way of relating to youth, their

families, and each other that conveys compassion, understanding, respect, and interest. Caring is also the source of the two other protective factors that help produce resilience in children and youth: positive and high expectations and opportunities for meaningful participation in school.

POSITIVE AND HIGH EXPECTATIONS

Schools that establish high expectations for all students—and provide the support necessary to achieve these expectations—have high rates of academic success (Brook, Nomura, and Cohen 1989; Edmonds 1986; Howard 1990; Levin 1988; Rutter et al. 1979; Slavin, Karweit, and Madden 1989). In their book *Fifteen Thousand Hours*, Rutter (1979) and his colleagues report on research that they conducted in schools located in some of the most poverty-ridden areas of London. Their findings show considerable differences in these schools' rates of delinquency, behavioral disturbance, attendance, and academic attainment (even after controlling for family "risk" factors). The successful schools shared certain characteristics: an emphasis on academics, clear expectations and regulations, high levels of student participation, and alternative resources such as library facilities, vocational work opportunities, art, music, and extracurricular activities. One of the most significant findings is that the longer students attend these successful schools, the more their problem behaviors decrease. In unsuccessful schools, the opposite is true—the longer students attend them, the more they exhibit problem behaviors. Rutter and colleagues (1979) concluded that, "Schools that foster high self-esteem and that promote social and scholastic success reduce the likelihood of emotional and behavioral disturbance" (p. 83).

Resiliency researcher Garmezy (1991) claims Rutter's work "stands forth as a possible beacon for illuminating the role of schools as a strategic force in fostering the well-being of disadvantaged children" (p. 425). The power of a schoolwide ethos of high expectations also appears in research on protective factors by Brook and her colleagues (Brook et al. 1989). This research team found that high expectations and a schoolwide ethos that values student participation mitigate powerful risk factors in adolescents' use of alcohol and drugs.

During the last decade, research on successful programs for youth at risk of academic failure has clearly demonstrated that high expectations—with concomitant support—is a critical factor in decreasing the number of students who drop out of school and in increasing the number of youth who go on to college (Mehan et al. 1994). For example, when a poor, inner-city school established a college core curriculum, more than 65 percent of its graduates went on to higher education—up from 15 percent before the program began. Several students in this program stated that "having one person who believed I could do it" was a major factor in their decision to attend college (California Department of Education 1990, p. 15). Similarly, Levin's Accelerated Schools Program and Slavin's Success for All project demonstrate that engaging low-achieving students in a challenging, speeded-up curriculum—as opposed to one that is slowed-down or remedial—produces positive academic and social outcomes (Levin 1988, Slavin et al. 1989). These findings are in direct contrast to the dismal achievement of children whose schools label them slow learners and track them into low-ability classes—high percentages being children of color—as documented in Oakes's (1985) study of tracking.

Conveying positive and high expectations to students occurs in several ways. One of the most obvious and powerful is through personal relationships in which teachers and other school staff communicate to students, "This work is important; I know you can do it; I won't give up on you" (Howard 1990).

An African-American woman recalls her schooling experience:

> I had a really second-rate education in junior high and high school. Most of my teachers were white. Their approach was to pat us on the back and tell us we were fine. Nothing was required. They just gave up on us. . . . Once I had a black teacher who was really tough—but I loved her because she *cared*. She even dared to flunk people. She made us do difficult tasks, made us think hard about what we were doing. The others thought we didn't need schooling because we'd never be anything anyway, so there was no need to worry about teaching (Delpit 1995, p. 119).

The literature on resiliency repeatedly confirms the protective power of firm guidance, challenge, and stimulus—plus loving support (Garbarino et al. 1992, Werner 1990). Youth who are succeeding against the odds talk of being respected and of having their strengths and abilities recognized (McLaughlin et al. 1994, Mehan et al. 1994). Successful teachers of poor children refuse to label their students "at risk"; they look at each child and see the gem that is inside and communicate this vision back to the child (Ashton-Warner 1963, Ayers 1993, Carini 1982, Curwin 1992, Heath 1983, Kohl 1967). They look for children's strengths and interests, and they use these as starting points for learning. The following words of a teacher whose whole classroom consists of linguistic and cultural minority students demonstrates her focus:

> I don't look at their past. Well, I do and I don't. I look at what I have in front of me. I know that there are a lot of things out there that are affecting their lives and you do have to think about that, but I also think that these are kids who love coming to school and they are ready to receive anything. I look at it as no one has any problem receiving information and processing just because they are so-called "mountain people" [from Laos and Cambodia].
>
> I think my students have potential, motivation. They're not turned off to anything. They have motivation from themselves and from the group. They have determination and will. They haven't been handed everything on the proverbial silver platter. Everything we do is new and great. . .[—] every book, every piece of art (Hauser and Thompson 1995, p. 213).

In *Among School Children*, Kidder (1990) describes the power that teachers have to motivate children: "For children who are used to thinking of themselves as stupid or not worth talking to or deserving rape and beatings, a good teacher can provide an astonishing revelation. A good teacher can give a child at least a chance to feel, 'She thinks I'm worth something; maybe I am'" (p. 3). Thus, a relationship that conveys high expectations to students can help them internalize these beliefs and by doing so develop the self-esteem and self-efficacy that Rutter found in the successful schools in his study.

Schools also communicate expectations in the way they structure and organize learning (Weinstein, Soule, Collins, Cone, Mehlorn, and Stimmonacchi 1991). We have already discussed the positive results that accrue from giving all youth access to college core subjects. Rutter's research also confirms that a rich and varied curriculum gives students the opportunity to be successful not just in academics but also in art, music, sports, community service, work apprenticeship, and helping their peers. Similarly, teachers who teach to a broad range of learning styles and multiple intelligences communicate that the school values the unique strengths and intelligences of each individual (Gardner 1985). Schools that encourage critical thinking and inquiry and the development of a critical consciousness are not only able to engage youth but are especially effective at communicating the expectation that students are truly capable of complex problem solving and decision making (Kohl 1994, Mehan et al. 1994).

Another strategy that leads to high expectations and resiliency is infusing multicultural content throughout the curriculum. This honors students' home cultures, gives them the opportunity to study their own and other cultures, and helps them develop cultural sensitivity. All children and youth need to develop their primary language skills and learn English as a second language or, if English is their primary language, to learn a second language. Moreover, schools must be adept at doing this without intensifying cultural and language stereotypes. As Hilliard (1989) concludes after years of studying the role of learning and teaching style in the education of youth of color, "The explanation for the low performance of culturally different minority group students will not be found by pursuing questions of behavioral style. . . . The children, no matter, what their style, are failing primarily because of systematic inequities in the delivery of whatever pedagogical approach the teachers claim to master—not because students cannot learn from teachers whose styles do not match their own" (p. 68). He goes on to discuss low expectations for youth of color as the core of these "systematic inequities."

How we group children in our classrooms and schools indicates the expectations we have for them. Research by Oakes (1985) and others documents the deleterious effects of tracking on low-achieving students. Conversely, recent research demonstrates the positive effects of untracked schools on students' aspirations. According to this research, all students, but especially low achievers, show positive academic and social outcomes as a result of heterogeneous, cooperative learning groups (Wheelock 1992, Johnson and Johnson 1990, Slavin 1990). Furthermore, no matter how well-meaning, targeted programs that label children at risk may be doing more harm than good. As educator Kohl tells it, "Although I've taught in East Harlem, in Berkeley, and in rural California, I have never taught an at-risk student in my life. The term is racist. It defines a child as pathological, based on what he or she might do rather than on anything he or she has actually done" (Nathan 1991, p. 679).

Evaluation is one more component of schooling through which we convey either high or low expectations. Schools that motivate young people to learn do not rely on standardized tests that assess only one or two types of intelligences, usually linguistic and logical-mathematical, according to Gardner (1985). Nor do they focus on "right answer" questions and assessments. Instead, they use several assessment approaches, including authentic assessments that promote student reflection, critical inquiry, and problem solving, and assessments that validate children's different intelligences, strengths, and learning styles.

A final area in which expectations play a role is in motivating students and instilling within them a responsibility for learning. Kohn (1993) argues that extrinsic rewards "punish" youth. Schools that are especially successful in promoting resiliency build on students' intrinsic motivation. These schools actively engage students in a variety of rich and experiential curriculums that connect to their interests, strengths, and real-world activities (Anderman and Maehr 1994, Weinstein et al. 1991). In addition, they count on students' active participation and decision making in the daily life of the classroom and school to build responsibility and ownership for learning. These, in turn, become intrinsic motivators for further learning and resiliency.

OPPORTUNITIES FOR MEANINGFUL PARTICIPATION IN SCHOOL

Providing opportunities for meaningful involvement and responsibility fosters resilience in a number of ways. Rutter (1984) found that schools that gave children a lot of responsibility had low levels of delinquency and dropouts. In these schools, children "participated very actively in all sorts of things that went on in the school; they were treated as responsible people and they reacted accordingly" (p. 65). Similarly, the High/Scope Educational Research Foundation's 15-year study of the Perry Preschool Project demonstrates the benefits of creating opportunities for children to participate in decision making from an early age. This study discovered that children from impoverished inner-city environments who planned and made decisions about their school activities in their preschool years were, at the age of 19, significantly less (as much as 50 percent) involved in using drugs, delinquency, teen pregnancy, or school failure (Berruta-Clement, Schweinhart, Barnett, Epstein, and Weikart 1984). A follow-up study of this population at age 27 found that participants in the project commit far fewer crimes, have higher earnings, and possess a greater commitment to marriage than other adults from similar backgrounds (Weikart and Schweinhart 1993).

In a recent study of the "turnaround" process, of how youths who were failing in school were able to become successful, one youth described how a community service project enabled him to engage and experience success:

> It was on an internship I did. You know, like, they liked the way I worked and they asked me if I could run a little youth group, if I want to do that, and I agreed to it. And then, in the beginning, I was just doing it so it could be on my resume and it could look good, but now I'm doing it because I like it and it, you know, became a big thing because I got everybody into it. Before I used to think just I'm messed up in high school and, you know, I'm just gonna sell drugs on the street corner, you know, just to make money. But now, like I already made up my mind what I want to be and I already know the steps I'm gonna take so, it'll be easy (Gregory 1995, p. 148).

Participating in decisions about one's life and future is a fundamental human need, closely tied to the need to have some power over one's life. Several educational reformers believe that ignoring this need—not only among children but also among families, teachers, and other school staff—makes schools alienating places (Glasser 1990, Wehlage et al. 1989). Sarason (1990) states it simply: "When one has no stake in the way things are, when one's needs are provided no forum, when one sees oneself as the object of unilateral actions, it takes no particular wisdom to suggest that one would rather be elsewhere" (p. 83).

The challenge for schools is to engage all children's innate desire and ability to learn by providing them with opportunities to participate in meaningful activities and roles. This is especially critical for students of color whose families and communities have been systematically excluded from fully participating in the social, economic, and political life of this country. Infusing opportunities for children to participate in the life of the classroom and school doesn't require a special program; it requires teachers to relinquish their role as "sage on the stage" and become the "guide on the side." Teachers must willingly share power with students and base their classrooms on reciprocity and collaboration instead of control and competition; in other words, the classroom must become a democratic community. Asking questions that encourage critical, reflective thinking (including those around current social problems); making learning more hands-on; involving students in curriculum planning; using participatory evaluation strategies; letting students create the "classroom constitution" (Sarason's [1990] term for agreements governing classroom interaction); and employing approaches like cooperative learning, peer helping, cross-age mentoring, and community service all give students opportunities for meaningful participation. Such strategies bond young people to their school community and promote all the traits of resiliency—social competence, problem solving, autonomy, and, especially critical to urban youth, a sense of a bright future (Benard 1991b, 1992; Kohn 1993).

Research demonstrates that a school climate characterized by caring, high expectations, and opportunities for students to participate in decision making is a powerful antidote to the risk factors in the lives of so many urban children. In his classic study on school effectiveness, Edmonds (1986) concluded that schools can create "coherent" environments and that these environments can affect students more than any single influence—teachers, class, family, or neighborhood. According to Edmonds, this environment is "so potent that for at least six hours a day it can override almost everything else in the lives of children."

What is increasingly apparent is that in order to create a climate conducive to student resiliency, we must create it for all school personnel. The need is for a school community in which everyone has a voice and an opportunity to share their gifts (Brandt 1992, Glasser 1990, Gibbs 1994, McLaughlin et al. 1994, Newmann 1994, Sarason 1990, Sergiovanni 1994, Wehmiller 1992). Sergiovanni (1994) writes,

"The need for community is universal. A sense of belonging, of continuity, of being connected to others and to ideas and values that make ourselves meaningful and significant—these needs are shared by all of us" (p. xiii). Building a school community also means, according to Wehmiller (1992), tearing down the walls that schools have built around them to keep out the families and communities of the "other" United States. She states, "To be inclusive, to be excellent, to be who we need to be as a whole community, everyone's truth must be known. Instead of a mission, schools need to create a covenant, . . .a promise to carry the gifts, the stories, the histories, the visions, the dreams of all the people inside the school. It is a promise to take down the walls of exclusion" (p. 381).

Building community and creating this covenant is the essence of fostering resiliency. It challenges us at both the personal and political levels. Personally, fostering resiliency is an inside-out, deep-structure process of changing our belief systems. It calls upon us to see resilience and not risk, strengths instead of deficits, and resources instead of problems in children and youth, their families, and their cultures. It requires, as Polakow (1993) says, "an ethic of caring—a change of heart and a change in our ways of seeing" (p. 182).

Successful restructuring to foster resiliency operates at this level of personal beliefs. As Hilliard (1991) eloquently writes, "To restructure we must first look deeply at the goals that we set for our children and the beliefs that we have about them. Once we are on the right track there, then we must turn our attention to the delivery systems, as we have begun to do. Untracking is right. Mainstreaming is right. Decentralization is right. Cooperative learning is right. Technology access for all is right. Multiculturalism is right. But none of these approaches or strategies will mean anything if the fundamental belief does not fit with new structures that are being created" (p. 36).

Furthermore, fostering resiliency in urban schools requires working politically for educational, social, and economic justice. Molnar (1994) says it well: "At their heart. . .the problems of city schools are the result of our failure to place school reform inside of a broader vision of social and economic justice and our unwillingness to engage in the kind of political activity necessary to realize that vision" (p. 59). Hope for our inner cities—which ultimately means hope for all of us—lies in engaging the innate resiliency, energy, and creativity of urban youth. It means welcoming youth to the "table" in our schools and communities. It means someday saying "Yes!" as a nation to ideas such as the peace plan created by youths in the rivaling Crips and Bloods gangs after the 1992 L.A. rebellion. That peace plan was a proposal to repair the streets and schools and to get rid of drugs and violence. The closing lines of their proposal: "Give us the hammers and the nails, and we will rebuild the city." Let's give them the chance.

REFERENCES

Anderman, E., and M. Maehr. (1994). "Motivation and Schooling in the Middle Grades." *Review of Educational Research* 64, 2: 287-309.

Ashton-Warner, S. (1963). *Teacher.* New York: Simon and Schuster.

Ayers, W. (1993). *To Teach: The Journey of a Teacher.* New York: Teachers College.

Barber, B. (November 1993). "America Skips School: Why We Talk So Much about Education and Do So Little." *Harper's Magazine*, 39-46.

Benard, B. (1990a). *The Case for Peers.* Portland, Ore.: Northwest Regional Educational Laboratory.

Benard, B. (1991a). *Fostering Resiliency in Kids: Protective Factors in the Family, School, and Community.* Portland, Ore.: Northwest Regional Educational Laboratory.

Benard, B. (1991b). *Moving Toward a Just and Vital Culture: Multiculturalism in Our Schools.* Portland, Ore.: Northwest Regional Educational Laboratory.

Benard, B. (1992). *Mentoring Programs for Urban Youth: Handle with Care.* Portland, Ore.: Northwest Regional Educational Laboratory.

Berruta-Clement, J., L. Schweinhart, W. Barnett, A. Epstein, and D. Weikart. (1984). *Changed Lives: The Effects of the Perry Preschool Program on Youths Through Age 19.* Ypsilanti, Mich.: High/Scope.

Brandt, R. (1992). "On Building Learning Communities: A Conversation with Hank Levin." *Educational Leadership* 50, 1: 19-23.

Brook, J., C. Nomura, and P. Cohen. (1989). "A Network of Influences on Adolescent Drug Involvement: Neighborhood, School, Peer, and Family." *Genetic, Social, and General Psychology Monographs* 115, 1: 303-321.

Butterworth, E. (1993). "Love: The One Creative Force." In *Chicken Soup*

for the Soul, edited by J. Canfield and M.V. Hansen. Deerfield,
Fla.: Health Communications.

California Department of Education. (1990). *Enhancing Opportunities for Higher Education Among Underrepresented Students*. Sacramento, Calif.: Author.

Carini, P. (1982). *The School Lives of Seven Children: A Five Year Study*. Grand Forks, N.D.: University of North Dakota.

Children's Defense Fund. (1994). *The State of America's Children Yearbook, 1994*. Washington, D.C.: Author.

Children's Express. (1993). *Voices from the Future: Children Tell Us About Violence in America*. New York: Crown.

Comer, J. (1984). "Home-School Relationships as They Affect the Academic Success of Children." *Education and Urban Society* 16, 3: 323-337.

Currie, E. (1993). *Reckoning: Drugs, the Cities, and the American Future*. New York: Hill and Wang.

Curwin, R. (1992). *Rediscovering Hope: Our Greatest Teaching Strategy*. Bloomington, Ind.: National Educational Service.

Delpit, L. (1995). *Other People's Children: Cultural Conflict in the Classroom*. New York: New Press.

Edmonds, R. (1986). "Characteristics of Effective Schools." In *The School Achievement of Minority Children: New Perspectives*, edited by U. Neisser. Hillsdale, N.J.: Lawrence Erlbaum.

Eggert, L., and J. Herting. (1991). "Preventing Teenage Drug Abuse: Exploratory Effects of Network Social Support." *Youth and Society* 22, 4: 482-524.

Erickson, F. (1987). "Transformation and School Success: The Politics and Culture of Educational Achievement." *Anthropology and Education Quarterly* 18, 4: 335-356.

Erikson, E. (1963). *Childhood and Society*. 2nd ed. New York: W.W. Norton.

Farrell, E. (1990). *Hanging In and Dropping Out: Voices of At-Risk High School Students*. New York: Teachers College.

Felner, R., M. Aber, J. Primavera, and A. Cauce. (1985). "Adaptation and Vulnerability in High-Risk Adolescents: An Examination of Environmental Mediators." *American Journal of Community Psychology* 13, 4:365-379.

Fine, M. (1991). *Framing Dropouts: Notes on the Politics of an Urban High School*. New York: State University of New York.

Gandara, P. (1995). *Over the Ivy Walls: The Educational Mobility of Low-Income Chicanos*. Albany, N.Y.: State University of New York Press.

Garbarino, J., N. Dubrow, K. Kostelny, and C. Pardo. (1992). *Children in Danger: Coping with the Consequences of Community Violence.* San Francisco, Calif.: Jossey-Bass.

Gardner, H. (1985). *The Frames of Mind: Theory of Multiple Intelligences.* New York: Basic Books.

Garmezy, N. (1991). "Resiliency and Vulnerability to Adverse Developmental Outcomes Associated with Poverty." *American Behavioral Scientist* 34, 4: 416-430.

Gibbs, J. (1994). *Tribes: A New Way of Learning Together.* Santa Rosa, Calif.: Center Source Publications.

Glasser, W. (1990). *The Quality School: Managing Students Without Coercion.* New York: Harper and Row.

Golarz, R., and M. Golarz. (1995). *The Power of Participation: Improving Schools in a Democratic Society.* Sebastopol, Calif.: National Training Associates.

Gregory, L. (1995). "The Turnaround Process: Factors Influencing the School Success of Urban Youth." *Journal of Adolescent Research* 10, 1: 148.

Hauser, M., and C. Thompson. (1995). "Creating a Classroom Culture of Promise: Lessons from a First Grade." In *Children and Families "at Promise": Deconstructing the Discourse of Risk*, edited by B.B. Swadener and S. Lubeck. New York: SUNY Press.

Heath, S.B. (1983). *Ways with Words.* New York: Cambridge University.

Heath, S.B., and M. McLaughlin, eds. (1993). *Identity and Inner-City Youth: Beyond Ethnicity and Gender.* New York: Teachers College.

Hetherington, M., M. Cox, and R. Cox. (1982). "Effects of Divorce on Parents and Children." In *Non-Traditional Families*, edited by M. Lamb. Hillsdale, N.J.: Lawrence Erlbaum.

Higgins, C. (1988). *Youth Motivation: At-Risk Youth Talk to Program Planners.* Philadelphia, Pa.: Public/Private Ventures.

Hilliard, A. (1991). "Do We Have the Will to Educate All Children?" *Educational Leadership* 49, 1: 31-36.

Hilliard, A. (1989). "Teachers and Cultural Styles in a Pluralistic Society." *NEA Today* 7, 6: 65-69.

Howard, J. (1990). *Getting Smart: The Social Construction of Intelligence.* Lexington, Mass.: The Efficacy Institute.

Institute for Education in Transformation. (1992). *Voices from the Inside: A Report on Schooling from Inside the Classroom.* Claremont, Calif.: Claremont Graduate School.

Johnson, D., and R. Johnson. (1990). *Learning Together and Alone.* New York: Prentice Hall.

Kagan, D. (1990). "How Schools Alienate Students At Risk: A Model for Examining Proximal Classroom Variables." *Educational Psychologist* 25, 2: 105-125.

Kellam, S. (December 3-4, 1982). "Social Adaptational and Psychological Antecedents in First Grade of Adolescent Psychopathology Ten Years Later. Preventive Aspects of Suicide and Affective Disorders among Adolescents and Young Adults." Paper presented at a research workshop, Harvard School of Public Health, Boston, Mass.

Kent, A. (June 1995). "The Power of Peer Helping." From the Fourth Annual UC Berkeley Incentive Awards Dinner Program and Activities Report, San Francisco, June, 18, 1995.

Kidder, T. (1990). *Among School Children*. New York: Avon.

Kohl, H. (1994). *"I Won't Learn from You" and Other Thoughts on Creative Maladjustment*. New York: The New Press.

Kohl, H. (1967). *Thirty-Six Children*. New York: New American Library.

Kohn, A. (1991). "Caring Kids: The Role of the Schools." *Phi Delta Kappan* 72, 7: 497-506.

Kohn, A. (1993). "Choices for Children: Why and How to Let Students Decide." *Phi Delta Kappan* 75, 1: 8-20.

Kozol, J. (1991). *Savage Inequalities: Children in America's Schools*. New York: Crown.

Lefkowitz, B. (1987). *Tough Change: Growing Up on Your Own in America*. New York: Doubleday.

Levin, H. (1988). "Accelerated Schools for Disadvantaged Students." *Educational Leadership* 44, 6: 19-21.

Lifton, R.J. (1993). *The Protean Self: Human Resilience in an Age of Fragmentation*. New York: Basic Books.

Maston, A. (1994). "Resilience in Individual Development: Successful Adaptation Despite Risk and Adversity." In *Educational Resilience in Inner City America: Challenges and Prospects*, edited by M.C. Wang, G.D. Haertel, and H.J. Walberg. Hillsdale, N.J.: Lawrence Erlbaum.

McLaughlin, M. (1990). "The Rand Change Agent Study Revisited: Macro Perspectives and Micro Realities." *Educational Researcher* 19, 9: 11-16.

McLaughlin, M., M. Irby, and J. Langman. (1994). *Urban Sanctuaries: Neighborhood Organizations in the Lives and Futures of Inner-City Youth*. San Francisco, Calif.: Jossey-Bass.

McLaughlin, M., and J. Talbert. (1993). *Contexts that Matter for Teaching and Learning*. Stanford, Calif.: Stanford University.

Mehan, H., L. Hubbard, and I. Villanueva. (1994). "Forming Academic Identities: Accommodation Without Assimilation Among Involuntary Minorities." *Anthropology and Education Quarterly* 25, 2: 91-117.

Miller, A. (1990). *The Untouched Key: Tracing Childhood Trauma in Creativity and Destructiveness*. New York: Anchor/Doubleday.

Molnar, A. (1994). "City Schools Under Attack." *Educational Leadership* 51, 8: 58-59.

Nathan, J. (May 1991). "An Interview with Herb Kohl: Toward Educational Change and Economic Justice." *Phi Delta Kappan* 72, 9: 678-681.

Newmann, F. (Spring 1994). "School-Wide Professional Community." *Issues in Restructuring Schools*, 1-6. Issue report no. 6.

Noddings, N. (December 7, 1988). "Schools Face Crisis in Caring." *Education Week*, p. 32.

Noddings, N. (1992). *The Challenge to Care in Schools: An Alternative Approach to Education*. New York: Teachers College.

NOW Legal Defense and Education Fund. (1988). *In Their Own Voices: Young Women Talk about Dropping Out*. Washington, D.C.: Author.

Oakes, J. (1985). *Keeping Track: How Schools Structure Inequality*. New Haven: Yale University.

Pearce, J.C. (1992). *Evolution's End: Claiming the Potential of Our Intelligence*. San Francisco, Calif.: Harper Collins.

Phelan, P., A. Davidson, and H.T. Cao. (May 1992). "Speaking Up: Students' Perspectives on School." *Phi Delta Kappan* 73, 9: 695-704.

Polakow, V. (1993). *Lives on the Edge: Single Mothers and Their Children in the Other America*. Chicago, Ill.: University of Chicago.

Rutter, M. (March 1984). "Resilient Children." *Psychology Today*, 57-65.

Rutter, M. (1985). "Resilience in the Face of Adversity: Protective Factors and Resistance to Psychiatric Disorder." *British Journal of Psychiatry* 147: 598-611.

Rutter, M., B. Maughan, P. Mortimore, J. Ouston, and A. Smith. (1979). *Fifteen Thousand Hours*. Cambridge, Mass.: Harvard University.

Sarason, S. (1990). *The Predictable Failure of Educational Reform*. San Francisco, Calif.: Jossey-Bass.

Schor, J. (1992). *The Overworked American: The Unexpected Decline of Leisure*. New York: Basic Books.

Sergiovanni, T. (1994). *Building Community in Schools*. San Francisco, Calif.: Jossey-Bass.

Slavin, R. (1990). *Cooperative Learning: Theory, Research, and Practice*. Englewood Cliffs, N.J.: Prentice Hall.

Slavin, R., N. Karweit, and N. Madden. (1989). *Effective Programs for Students At Risk.* Boston, Mass.: Allyn and Bacon.

Stevenson, R., and J. Ellsworth. (1993). "Drop-Outs and the Silencing of Critical Voices." In *Beyond Silenced Voices: Class, Race, and Gender in United States Schools,* edited by L. Weis and M. Fine. New York: State University of New York.

Wallerstein, J., and S. Blakeslee. (1990). *Second Chances: Men, Women, and Children a Decade after Divorce.* Bloomington, Ind.: Ticknor and Fields.

Wehlage, G., R. Rutter, G. Smith, N. Lesko, and R. Fernandez. (1989). *Reducing the Risk: Schools as Communities of Support.* Philadelphia, Pa.: Falmer.

Wehmiller, P.L. (1992). "When the Walls Come Tumbling Down." *Harvard Educational Review* 62, 3: 373-383.

Weikart, D., and L. Schweinhart. (1993). *Significant Benefits: The High/ Scope Perry Preschool Study Through Age 27.* Ypsilanti, Mich.: Educational Resource Foundation.

Weinstein, R., C. Soule, F. Collins, J. Cone, M. Mehlorn, and K. Stimmonacchi. (1991). "Expectations and High School Change: Teacher-Researcher Collaboration to Prevent School Failure." *American Journal of Community Psychology* 19, 3: 333-363.

Weis, L., and M. Fine, eds. (1993). *Beyond Silenced Voices: Class, Race, and Gender in United States Schools.* New York: State University of New York.

Werner, E. (1990). "Protective Factors and Individual Resilience." In *Handbook of Early Childhood Intervention,* edited by S. Meisels and J. Shonkoff. New York: Cambridge University.

Werner, E., and R. Smith. (1989). *Vulnerable but Invincible: A Longitudinal Study of Resilient Children and Youth.* New York: Adams, Bannister, and Cox.

Werner, E., and R. Smith. (1992). *Overcoming the Odds: High-Risk Children from Birth to Adulthood.* New York: Cornell University.

Wheelock, A. (1992). *Crossing the Tracks: How "Untracking" Can Save America's Schools.* New York: W.W. Norton.

Wilson, W.J. (1987). *The Truly Disadvantaged: The Inner City, the Underclass, and Public Policy.* Chicago: University of Chicago.

7

Teacher Engagement and Real Reform in Urban Schools[1]

KAREN SEASHORE LOUIS AND BETSANN SMITH

Two facts about public education in the 21st century are inescapable: The student population will become increasingly multicultural, and students will come from families of lower socioeconomic status. These demographic shifts challenge schools to mount massive reforms that range from providing onsite social services to developing new curriculums that spark learning among new generations of students.

How these demographic shifts affect teachers has received much less attention than the need to address changing student characteristics. This chapter considers the prospects for improving teacher engagement in urban schools through professional and organizational reform. It argues that creating a teaching force with the energy and skill to instruct today's urban students requires more than matching students and teachers or improving the skills of individual educators. Rather, it is a matter of creating schools where all teachers are learners together with their colleagues (Lieberman 1988, Senge 1990). The systemic reform literature (Fuhrman 1993) argues that real improvement in schools will not occur unless teachers' professional development more clearly focuses on specific student learning outcomes and a common curriculum. However, skills and knowledge will not be enough unless other aspects of teachers' work also improve. In particular, the changing conditions of schools decrease traditional intrinsic rewards for teachers and increase uncertainty, which in turn reduces teachers' commitment to and engagement in their work. Yet as research reported here will indicate, modest changes in the conditions under which urban teachers work can make dramatic differences in their engagement.

URBAN EDUCATION AS A SPECIAL CONTEXT FOR TEACHING

> The conditions in some of our schools are so bad, and the physical and social environments in which these schools are located are so frightful, that we may have to cross off some . . . as expendable (Halpin 1966, as quoted in Englert 1993, p. 3).

Creating high-quality working environments for teachers is an issue in all schools, but it is particularly problematic in large cities. The reasons include socioeconomic, political, and organizational conditions that, while not unique, converge to make urban schools both vulnerable and demanding places for teachers.

SOCIOECONOMIC CONDITIONS

The social and economic characteristics of urban communities have significant implications for teachers' work. The problems that their students bring to school may overwhelm urban teachers, making it more difficult for them to successfully engage with normal issues of pedagogy. Moreover, the double disadvantage of poor students and poor communities puts a particular strain on teachers who are often from different socioeconomic backgrounds than their students yet must organize a pedagogy that will engage and connect the classroom to students' own experiences.

Urban schools also are harder to reform because many of them have weak links to the natural professional networks that diffuse ideas. During the mid-80s, only a tiny fraction of urban schools based any major change efforts on the then-popular "effective schools" literature (Louis and Miles 1990), which suggests that they were not well connected to the many change agents who promoted these principles at the time. Many major schools of education have recently developed "professional practice" relationships with local schools, but few of these are in major urban districts.

The socioeconomic setting also may limit internal human resources. Rollow and Bryk (1995) note that the Chicago Public School System is staffed largely by teachers who went through that system, who received their teacher training locally, and have taught in no other district. In part, this is because urban systems like to "hire their own." Teachers who are not familiar with the inner city also prefer to work in more affluent systems.

POLITICAL CONDITIONS

In urban settings, interest group politics mix with educational politics in a more volatile way than in smaller towns (Peterson 1985), and this also affects teachers' work. As Louis (1991a) notes, many urban settings display fragmented values concerning education, and, in particular, they are more likely to exhibit distance or even antagonism between the professional values of teachers and the concerns of parents and community members.

Recent restructuring efforts in major cities have almost uniformly revealed deep-seated differences between proponents of parental control over schooling and professional educators. There is more likely to be antagonism between professional educators and urban parents, and there are more parent and community groups that form distinctive perspectives of what should happen to schools.

Urban communities are often ethnically and racially heterogeneous, so "the community" also may be deeply divided. When this diversity is present in a school it can negatively affect decentralized school improvement efforts (Bryk, Easton, Kerbow, Rollow, and Sebring 1993). Under these conditions, many urban districts show the attributes of a "policy vacuum"—an absence of clear, organized constituencies; no clear understanding of policy issues and choices; little if any consistency in policy initiatives; and little coordination between overlapping or complementary policies (Corwin and Louis 1982). Policy vacuums lead to unstable educational policies, which also undermine school and teacher efforts to reform (Louis and Miles 1990).

ORGANIZATIONAL CONDITIONS

Almost by definition, urban school districts are large, and urban schools are larger than average schools. Recent efforts to look at the combined effects of district and school size suggest that big is more bureaucratic and bad for children—at least where students are of lower-socioeconomic status (Wahlberg 1989). For teachers, however, there is an added problem. Larger schools in lower socioeconomic communities tend to develop a lesser "sense of community" among teachers than do other schools (Bryk and Driscoll 1988), and sense of community goes hand-in-hand with student achievement (Lee and Smith 1994).

Creating an engaged teaching force that focuses on the common problems of teaching demands a great deal of the faculty, yet urban schools have more difficulty than others in recruiting and retaining the most talented teachers (Englert 1993). Urban teachers participate less in policy decisions, administrators treat them with less respect, they have fewer opportunities to engage in significant work with each other, and they are generally subject to unprofessional working conditions (Corcoran, Walker, and White 1988).

The nature of work in urban schools is, in addition, hurried, focused on the short term, and subject to interruption. Few teachers and administrators are easily able to be "reflective practitioners" who eagerly seek complex information to improve their work. Instead, they are often harassed and looking for information that will solve today's problem—today. Unfortunately, urban districts rarely have information management systems that allow them to gain access to usable data, much less information and ideas that are less familiar (Cibulka 1992).

TEACHER ENGAGEMENT AND STUDENT ACHIEVEMENT

Reformers attribute the problems of student learning to "bad" or "poorly prepared" teachers, but evidence suggests that an equally if not more serious problem is an increasing level of teachers' detachment and alienation from their work and students (National Education Association 1987, Corcoran et al. 1988, Metz 1990). From the student's point of view, teacher engagement is a prerequisite for student engagement; and from the teacher's point of view, student engagement is, in turn, the most important predictor of teachers' interest and effort. In this sense, teacher engagement is a subset of the broader objective of creating effective schools that increase student learning opportunities and improve student achievement.

TEACHERS' DEPENDENCE ON STUDENTS: THE "IRON LAW OF SOCIAL CLASS"

If teachers depend for their professional satisfaction only on students' increasing mastery of the classroom material, is the only way to increase teacher professionalism to get better students?

Teachers get psychic rewards from watching their students learn. Dedicated teachers point with pride to students who have made progress on particular concepts this week or who have picked up a whole range of cognitive skills that they did not have at the beginning of the year. Seeing the results of their efforts is, for teachers, as important as it is for physicians to see patients getting well or for lawyers to see clients' lives changed because of their interventions.

But learning is not equally distributed among students, and neither is teachers' sense of efficacy in their work. Research suggests a strong correlation between students' socioeconomic characteristics and teachers' satisfaction and engagement with teaching (Firestone and Rosenblum 1988, Metz 1990, Dworkin 1987, Brookover et al. 1979).[2]

Compared with teachers of more affluent children, teachers who work with students from poorer families are more likely, for example, to believe that their students bring behaviors into the classroom that make teaching difficult. They also tend to believe that they have little influence over their students' learning. In addition, teachers in schools with a higher proportion of minority children are more likely to feel unrewarded for their teaching efforts when their students do not engage in learning. Is it not surprising, then, that we find many teachers claiming, "If you only gave me students who were prepared to learn, I could be a great teacher!"

Here is the Catch 22. Unless teachers engage in teaching and feel that they are effective, students are less likely to make rapid progress in learning. And from the student's point of view, teacher engagement is a prerequisite for student engagement. This is particularly true for schools with a high concentration of lower income and minority students (Bryk and Thum 1989; Wehlage, Rutter, Lesko, and Fernandez 1989; Brookover et al. 1979; Wilson and Corcoran 1988).[3] Because teachers' work and students' work are linked, alienated teachers pose a major stumbling block to students' engagement with their own education (Lee and Smith 1994).[4]

In traditionally organized schools, teachers' lives revolve almost exclusively around their classroom. It is not surprising that these teachers work with the most responsive and quickest students, predominantly from the middle classes and on higher tracks. Such students reinforce teachers' professional satisfactions.[5]

The research presented here, however, offers a different perspective: While it is not possible to change students' social origins, it may be possible to change the relationship between social class and teacher commitment and engagement in the right organizational conditions. The purpose of our research (Louis and Smith 1991) was to see whether it was possible to release teachers from an unhealthy "ultimate dependency" on their students by increasing the alternative sources of satisfaction and fulfillment (Barnard 1938).[6] Thus, rather than viewing teacher engagement solely as a function of student engagement, we sought to connect teacher engagement and the organizational conditions of the school. In doing so we acknowledged that success with students is fundamental to teacher satisfaction.

WHAT IS TEACHER ENGAGEMENT?

Unengaged teachers have been described as bored teachers who just go through the textbook and aren't thinking, teachers nicknamed "Mrs. Ditto, or Mr. Filmstrip," teachers who "taught one year, for 30 years" and teachers "who barely know their student's names."

Teacher engagement falls into four distinctive types. Two types are *affective* and focus on human relationships in the school, and two types are *instrumental* and focus on the goals of teaching and learning (Bryk and Driscoll 1988; Firestone and Rosenblum 1988; Wehlege, Rutter, Lesko, and Fernandez 1989).[7] Each form of engagement is desirable and must be present for teaching to remain vital and effective for all students. Thus, redesigning the school organization so that teachers of disadvantaged children enjoy the same opportunities for engagement as teachers of more advantaged children is fundamental to improving education.

• **Engagement with the school as a social unit.** This form of engagement reflects a sense of community and personal caring among adults within the school, and it promotes integration between personal life and work life. We see this form of engagement among teachers who "wouldn't want to work at any other school." These teachers refer to peers and students as friends and family, and they attend after-hours school events as often as they can. They are quick to rally together if faced with a troubling event.

• **Engagement with students as unique, whole individuals rather than as "empty vessels to be filled."** Teachers demonstrate this type of engagement when they listen to students' ideas, get involved in students' personal as well as school lives, and make themselves available to students who need support or assistance. Other examples of teacher engagement with students are formal and informal coaching, sponsoring, mentoring, and counseling activities.

• **Engagement with academic achievement.** Teachers can engage in students' achievement in many ways. They can participate in curriculum writing and development, share ideas and experiences about the craft of teaching with other teachers, make good and creative use of class time, express high expectations for performance, provide useful feedback to students, and actively consider student assessment.

• **Engagement with a body of knowledge needed to carry out effective teaching.** Particularly in secondary schools, teachers need to keep current in their content fields and incorporate new subject matter into instruction. Expressing one's personal passion for a subject, seeking ways to connect the subject to students lives, participating in professional organizations, and pursuing advanced degrees exemplify this form of engagement.

Most teachers, when they enter the profession, engage with their work along multiple dimensions. Over time, the presence and absence of various demands affects their engagement. There are demands teachers place on themselves as well as demands of their students, peers, principal, and parents—not to mention the immediate demands of the school environment. While demands may be stressful, they also can energize. Students who ask for more, and parents who involve themselves in the school, create an environment of high expectations for teachers.

In order to sustain their engagement, however, teachers (like students) need *positive reinforcers* that are consistent, meaningful, and rewarding (Newmann 1992). The four types of engagement are distinct, but the same structures and activities can reinforce several of them at the same time. For example, a staff development retreat on cooperative learning can develop a sense of community among adults while simultaneously focusing on student achievement.

According to some popular case studies, the most unpromising contexts—where demands on teachers are low and positive reinforcers limited—can still generate teacher engagement. Often, friendships among the faculty are the basis of such engagement (Kidder 1989, Freedman 1990). But teachers engaged only in a few dimensions do not necessarily serve students well. Staff may highly engage with the social community of adults in their school but neglect students' achievement. Or, they may become so obsessed with achievement that they remain distant from teachers of less able students. Dramatic imbalances such as these can be counterproductive to a school's functioning. We will argue below that demands and positive reinforcers often vary in schools of different socioeconomic climates in ways that disadvantage teachers of lower socioeconomic students.

PROFILES OF URBAN SCHOOLS WITH HIGH ENGAGEMENT

From 1987 to 1990, we conducted research in eight public, nonselective high schools actively involved in reform (Louis and Smith 1991b).[8] We chose a diverse sample of community environments from different regions of the country. One school was in a predominantly affluent community; three schools—one suburban, one rural, and one urban—were in mixed socioeconomic communities; and four schools served communities where over half of the students came from poor, minority, and immigrant families. Here we illustrate how three schools serving disadvantaged students created working conditions for teachers similar to those in schools that serve more advantaged students.

The schools are referred to here by pseudonym.[9] These three schools had the least affluent student bodies of the eight schools in the study. However, survey data measures indicated that the average staff member's level of engagement was as high as or higher than in the more affluent schools, although their working conditions (according to them) were worse.[10] These educators brought effort, energy, and hope to their teaching tasks in excess of what one might expect. Particularly striking was that teacher engagement in the three schools was higher than in two other schools where, although most of the students were from minority and non-English speaking populations, more students came from middle class homes. Thus, we believe that the schools' racial composition was not particularly important.

We begin by describing each school below, followed by a more detailed look at how these urban schools organized to increase teacher engagement.

CITY PARK SECONDARY SCHOOL

City Park is a small, innovative secondary school located in an impoverished section of a major northeastern city. It sits in the shadow of a public housing project where poverty, crime, drugs, and violence touch community members' lives daily. The school shares a large 1950s era building with two other small schools. The district allows high school parents and students to choose which school students

will attend. Although the immediate neighborhood is largely Hispanic, the school aims for a diverse enrollment and has largely suc-
ceeded. Its student body is approximately 45 percent black,
35 percent Hispanic, and 20 percent white. Students show a broad
range of academic ability.

The school has roots in the progressive education tradition. It sub-
scribes to the following principles:

• minimization of bureaucracy;

• a humanistic, open environment characterized by equal respect
for staff and students (for example, students do not need passes to go
to the bathroom, and students and staff members address each other
by their first names);

• no tracking;

• a core curriculum planned and developed by teams of teachers;

• significant team planning time;

• instructional and learning strategies oriented around "essential
questions" and inquiry;

• parent involvement; and

• an overall sense of family.

The school enrolls around 600 students in three divisions: 7-8,
9-10, and 11-12. These are further divided into houses with about 80
students each. There are no traditional departments. Instead, each division has a Math-Science Team and a Humanities Team, each consist-
ing of about five teachers. Teams meet weekly for two hours to
develop and coordinate curriculum, share ideas, and discuss what
has and has not worked. Scheduling is nontraditional, with students
and teachers meeting for two-hour blocks. Because of the division
structure, students stay with the same teachers for two years. They
also have the same advisor throughout their high school years. A
daily one-hour advisory period focuses on guidance for academic
and personal growth and reinforces the "family" atmosphere of the
school.

BRIGHAM ALTERNATIVE HIGH SCHOOL

Unlike City Park, Brigham is the only alternative school in its
small southern city. Established four years ago, the school seeks to
emphasize "open education" values that stress an interdisciplinary

curriculum and student responsibility for learning. Because it is the only "school of choice," Brigham has struggled with its image as a "dumping ground" to which other schools in the district send their most troubled and least successful students. Eighty percent of the student body is black. Most students are from working class or very poor families.

The school's educational philosophy revolves around experiential and cooperative learning, mixed ability grouping, a humanistic curriculum, and an informal environment. However, a rigid outcome-based district curriculum and testing program, known as CBOK (Common Body of Knowledge), inhibits the implementation of this philosophy, as does a local culture that still strongly supports "paddling" as a form of student discipline.

The school follows a traditional organization, with department heads, 50-minute periods, and age grouping. Some departments have grade-related teams so that a small number of teachers can become more familiar with all of the students, thus permitting easier monitoring of student performance and personal problems. The school also uses an advisory period for some guidance work, as well as to give students and teachers an opportunity for more personal interaction. Several committees share in the school's governance.

HILLSIDE HIGH SCHOOL

Hillside is located only a few miles from a medium-sized city. Its hilly setting appears remarkably bucolic, but a court-ordered district desegregation plan changed Hillside into an "urban school" virtually overnight. Unlike City Park and Brigham, Hillside is a long-established and large (more than 1,000 students) comprehensive high school with a traditional curriculum delivered by 13 departments in a 6-period day.

The community is one of the oldest in the state, but it has never prospered and remains sparsely settled. Several large industrial complexes have either closed or cut back their work forces, which has led to high levels of unemployment. The community's educational level is low, with a graduation rate in recent years of only about 65 percent. Only 30 percent of the graduates go on to some form of postsecondary education. Three-quarters of the student body are "local rednecks"—a term students and staff use freely; one quarter are African Americans bused in from the city.

Only five years ago, Hillside was considered one of the worst schools in the district; now teachers wait to transfer in. A local professional teacher academy has stimulated major reform efforts in the school. More recently, the school joined Ted Sizer's Coalition of Essential Schools. A staff vote approved establishing ties with both the local academy and Sizer's Coalition. The principal strongly supports both moves. The most critical change that these initiatives brought was the establishment of a steering committee composed of elected faculty members, the principal, the assistant principal, a counselor, the athletic director, representatives from the district's teacher center, students, parents, and an elected member of the nonprofessional support staff. This committee works primarily in subcommittees to develop new directions for Hillside. The steering committee has introduced programs such as teacher-guided assistance, daily periods when teachers help students with academic problems or issues; multidisciplinary curriculum units; and a "9th grade bridge" that employs an interdisciplinary curriculum and team teaching for approximately one-third of the incoming freshman class who appear most likely to drop out.

HOW THREE URBAN SCHOOLS ORGANIZE TO INCREASE TEACHER ENGAGEMENT

All three of these schools—City Park, Brigham, and Hillside—increased teacher engagement by paying close attention to three areas: school culture, organization, and leadership.

SCHOOL CULTURE

The schools share norms and values that make their teachers' work lives different from their colleagues in conventional schools. This has had a significant positive impact on teacher engagement.

A Strong Sense of Being in "A School with a Mission." A mission and vision create social pressures and psychological rewards for teachers who commit to the school and its version of educational excellence.

Teachers in all three schools emphasized the importance of being part of a school that had (or was striving for) a collective definition of its goals (high achievement) and strategies for reaching them. A teacher at Brigham spoke for most of her colleagues when she said: "I was attracted to this school because of the philosophy . . . . I was approached by a faculty member here . . . plus I had worked with the principal before . . . . We had the same ideas about education."

In City Park, where the pedagogical approach was most clearly articulated, many faculty mentioned the need to both live the mission and draw energy from it: "People know that . . . if you want to work in this school, [the team approach] is the bottom line . . . . I think [it] makes the job of teaching a creative experience, and creativity feeds on itself."

And at Hillside, where faculty were still struggling with the nature of their school's "special quality," there was a strong sense of taking part in a risky but exciting joint venture. As one physical education teacher said: "My personal goals, as far as teaching, go along with this school . . . . And after 23 years of teaching, to have that freedom to do some things, and the fact that I do not work alone anymore, that I work with a group of people, made it so much easier."

Developing or being part of a collective vision of education demands commitment. As one City Park teacher put it when asked about teaching somewhere else, "There *is* nowhere else to teach." Teachers at Hillside and Brigham also reported on the importance of collective commitment and the difficulty this sometimes posed for more individualistic teachers. But even some of these teachers, they say, "converted": "[Some] of the people . . . that I never thought would come 'on board' . . . have finally come around and have started working on things because they felt like they've wanted to and they needed to."

An Emphasis on Closeness Among Staff Members. In urban schools with high teacher commitment, staff emphasize the need to support each other, both personally and professionally. At Brigham, teachers often used "family" imagery to describe this special quality: "Sure, this is what we stress here, this family group, this closeness . . . . We are trying to be close to each other [as teachers], and know each other."

In City Park, there was a lot of talk about trust: " When I came here . . . I had to learn a lot. I got a tremendous amount of help. [The principal] helped me; [another teacher] with 14 years of experience became my best friend here . . . . I used to meet him every morning to talk about what we were going to do and how we were going to do it . . . and he would come observe my classes."

At Hillside, teachers expressed similar sentiments, with the most frequent being, "Everyone here is supportive."

An Emphasis on Respect and Caring for Students. "Part of teaching is lending your ego for a kid to learn . . . . If you are only teaching a subject [you're] not teaching kids," noted a teacher from City Park. Noddings (1992) has written extensively about the role that respect and caring play in teachers' work. A teacher from City Park best summarizes the way in which care intertwines with teacher and student engagement: "[If] you are teaching the kids, you see where each kid is and what their next step is. You have to perceive all of the differences . . . [,] you have to handle the resistance so that they may make steps for themselves . . . . You have to do that. That is an engaging process."

At Hillside, students talked openly about teachers' caring: "[They're] out to help you. They want you to learn. They will also sit down with you a lot of time, I mean work personally [with you]. It seems like they'll do it all the time, you know, to make sure you understand it."

Brigham made caring and the affirmation of individual worth critical features of its school vision. Caring gave teachers a sense of self-worth as well: "[This school] emphasizes self-worth. And if you can encourage, or you're successful in helping and enabling a person to feel good about themselves and about what they are doing, then the opportunity for that person to be a successful person is enhanced significantly . . . . We *are* doing that."

Caring is good for students, of course, but it is also good for teachers. Caring makes schools into ethical and moral environments, not just arenas for "getting the job done." Studies of beginning teachers indicate that the desire to be involved with the profession has a moral character. This is more than altruism. Teachers need to be engaged with work that has significance.

A Demand for Active Problem Solving Among Teachers. The most powerful form of empowerment that urban teachers encounter is the sense of being responsible for unearthing and solving problems. This theme emerged repeatedly in the three schools.

At City Park, one teacher commented about how student-teacher relationships reflected problem solving: "The assumption is that the kids are basically trying to do the best that they can, and that might not be so great at a given point in time, and you try to get everybody together and acknowledge that there's a problem. Rather than trying to blame someone, you try to deal with the problem, what are the different factors, and what can we do to change the situation. And that's the way problems are dealt with, even academically."

Hillsdale and Brigham also emphasized problem solving. Teachers there were responsible for managing their own environment. One new teacher explained: "If you have an idea [you go to the principal] and usually, if you give her your idea she will say, 'and how do you plan to put this idea into action?'"

We observed another new teacher remarking to her colleagues in a meeting: "You're all talking about what you want to accomplish at school . . . . At every other school I've ever been in they would be complaining and whining and griping and saying how bad the administration is. You all are figuring out what you're going to do—that's good, and it's really different."

Even in Brigham, which was located in a very centralized district, teachers actively looked for and solved problems: "[My] husband, who teaches in one of the other high schools . . . [,] he's surprised that [we] are allowed to make decisions that stick[—]. . . you know, about teacher time, teacher responsibility . . . ."

We should note that all of the schools expected teachers to help maintain constructive human relations at all times and all places. As one teacher related, "I used to walk past two kids rolling around on the floor, having a fight. That wasn't my business, that was up to the security guards. That doesn't happen here. Everything that happens is everybody's business. After all, in your house, if your kids are acting crazy, your husband doesn't wait until you get home!"

As a consequence of such active problem solving by teachers, disciplinary problems were, for the most part, rare.

Peer Pressure to Work. Peer pressure, when coupled with valued professional feedback, increases teacher engagement. Teachers do their best work when they collaborate with demanding colleagues. Of course, collaboration also exposes weaknesses, but other norms, especially teachers helping one another, cushion the potential negative impact of this.

Life in the three schools was more demanding than in most schools—but worth it. As one Brigham teacher said: "[The] teachers [who] have left here and gone to other places in the district . . . have said 'gosh, I miss it.' They go to the room and they work. And after school the bell rings and they hit the cars."

Another remarked: "We have had meetings [at this school] where we went through cooperative learning until 5:30 . . . but at [school x], no one helped . . . . And when I worked at [school y,] . . . each teacher was out for themselves."

City Park teachers talked about being exhausted and feeling that the process of curriculum development and active teaching had no end. But no teachers suggested that they wanted to leave. A Hillside teacher commented,

> "I do a lot more work and spend a lot more hours here, and I have to get along with a lot more people, but I enjoy it more and so it is worth it."

Why is pressure to work so engaging? It is engaging because it is tied to a sense of doing important work that has payoff for students who otherwise would be uninterested in school. At Hillside, experienced teachers expressed amazement about the differences in their students: "My biggest ego booster this year has been several teachers who have come to me and said, 'You know what? I've got some kids in my class that took your program last year, and they are better prepared than the rest of the kids in the class.' That has happened three or four times from three or four different teachers and that really makes me feel good."

SCHOOL ORGANIZATION

Although professional culture is at the heart of teacher engagement, school organization reinforces (or revives) staff commitments to teaching.

Creating Structures to Promote Teacher Decision Making. When teachers take part in making important decisions, they are active problem solvers. Principals in these schools did more than hold informal, open-door discussions with teachers. They built formal decision-making structures. While teachers valued informal opportunities to express their opinions or to make suggestions, the existence of formal decision-making bodies was a more important symbol of their professionalism. At Brigham, "We have the opportunity to influence things that are going on, such as electing the assistant principal. We have the opportunity to come up with meaningful plans and implement them."

At City Park, the faculty saw the entire school structure as designed for empowerment: "We are a decision-making school. We work as a whole school, we work . . . within our team and . . . within our classrooms where even kids are allowed to make some decisions about how things are to be done."

At Hillside, the steering-group structure worked well for teachers because it was tied to the kinds of curriculum renewal that were at the heart of their interests.

Creating Structures to Promote Collaboration. In all three schools, teachers linked high levels of engagement to spending more time with each other. Changing the way schools use time is one of the most difficult tasks of school reform. Two of these schools had restructured to give teachers more time to work together, while in the third, peer pressure made teachers put in extensive after-school time on collaborative work. This not only strengthened personal bonds, but it also infused new enthusiasm into instruction. City Park's schedule makes time for a weekly two-hour meeting in which teams develop curriculums, teaching strategies, and student assignments. The schedule reflects the value the school places on teachers' engagement with the academic program:

> "In my other school, what I was good at, I stayed good at. What I wasn't good at, I never improved . . . . I really could have been in the building all by myself. There were never times when you could get together and discuss issues with other teachers."

At Hillside, collaborations usually revolve around task-force work, or time spent in groups at the district's professional development center. (Both were made possible by the use of substitutes). In Brigham, the lack of resources and the school's inability to change district-imposed schedules made collaboration difficult. The school was extensively involved in the development of cooperative learning, but other collaborations had to be more informal. Still, teachers did not feel isolated. A Brigham teacher said: "I have found . . . professional collegiality presented here that my husband does not benefit from even though he's been at his school for 20 years. . . . I mean, I have teachers on their off period come by and sit in my classroom that are not even in the English department."

A Hillside staff member pointed to the link between collaboration and engagement: "We work together on so many things (because of the steering committee). And one of the things that has opened up is that if I want to do something within math, there are teachers here that I know I can go to and they will help me teach that in my classroom."

In City Park, the principal had a philosophy of collaboration that tied teacher engagement to student engagement: "You must remove teachers from isolation and make learning exciting. To make learning exciting for students, you must make learning exciting for teachers, because when learning is exciting for both teachers and students, kids can't get lost."

Creating Structures to Promote Professional Development. To increase teacher engagement, urban schools must become learning centers for professional staff as well as for students. Collegiality boosts engagement, in part because it increases interpersonal knowledge and the "family" feeling. This, in turn, enhances the development of professional competence. At Hillside, with its enormous resources and new enthusiasm for change, teachers viewed each day as an occasion to learn from others. As one teacher remarked: "There is tremendous opportunity to develop your skills and knowledge (in part) because of the collegiality that is so very prevalent. I mean, if you want to do it, there are people in this building that will do it with you. If you just want to sit back and be an observer, they'll let you come in and observe."

Another remarked that:

> "Probably the nicest thing about being here at this school
> is the opportunity to use and/or develop skills and knowl-
> edge. And we do a lot of inservice giving. I mean, a lot of our
> faculty members give inservices to others."

Teachers at Hillside and City Park viewed their schoolwide re-
treats as critical for both personal and collaborative development. Yet,
none of the schools considered the days officially dedicated to staff
development as important as the time spent on ad hoc or
semiplanned development opportunities. A teacher from City Park
summarizes the importance of continuing experimentation and skill
development: "[We're] not always doing the same thing. There's always something new to be thinking about . . . [;] it encourages you to
think about issues, to grapple with important questions."

Creating Structures to Improve Curriculum. Giving teachers the support they need to write curriculum specifically for the students they
teach can increase engagement. The problem of curriculum in urban
settings is profound. Investigators have found that inner-city teachers
often spend their energies on curriculums that are of questionable
benefit to students. They either teach a traditional college prepara-
tory curriculum to students who lack basic skills or, conversely, they
teach nothing but basic skills (Louis and Smith 1991).[11]

Teachers had autonomy over curriculum in all of the schools we
studied except Brigham. There, the school had only recently been re-
leased from rigid district controls. Even at Brigham, however, teachers spoke of how they "worked hard to make [the curriculum] ours,"
by introducing, for example, interdisciplinary perspectives. In the
three schools discussed here, teachers developed curriculums, instructional units, lesson plans, and instructional designs in teams.

The purpose of City Park's weekly team meetings was to develop
curriculums and to discuss instruction. Hillside had both departmen-
tal and cross-departmental curriculum teams. We have already described how collaborative group experiences benefit teachers.
Curriculum writing, in particular, encourages teachers to think about
and discuss fundamental issues of knowledge and learning. Moreover, it enables teachers to calculate the level of knowledge and the
kind of instruction that are best for the students they teach. That proc-

ess engages teachers with their students, with the school's academic program, with the craft of teaching, and with the subjects they teach.

SCHOOL LEADERSHIP

There was consensus among teachers that a school with an ineffective principal was unlikely to be exciting no matter how talented the staff. Teachers also agreed schools can become exciting quite rapidly after the arrival of a supportive principal. So far, we have discussed several features of school culture and organization that promote teacher engagement. Now we turn to the origins of these positive features.

Brigham and City Park were new schools; most teachers had chosen to work there. This created a sense of being in a special place and of working with a special team. On the other hand, most teachers had worked at Hillside for more than a decade. Until recently, few thought of it as unique. Now, teacher engagement at Hillside is nearly as high as at Brigham and City Park. The factor that all three schools have in common is leadership that promotes engagement. An effective principal facilitates a culture in which teacher engagement can flourish.

Buffering Teachers. Studies of conventional schools show that the principal often buffers teachers from unwanted interventions by parents (Rossmiller 1992).[12] In these three schools, however, principals encourage teachers to develop respectful relationships with parents regardless of parents' social position. They invite parents and community into the school. Two of the principals, however, did have to work very hard to protect their staff members from demands made by district offices. At Brigham and City Park, districts did not always support teacher autonomy. These principals recognized that teachers struggled to preserve their limited energies for students and teaching. Having principals who cared so deeply about protecting teachers' time was in itself a factor that increased many teachers' engagement.

Spending Time on Daily Routines. Leadership in the eight schools did not conform to the image of the efficient executive who participates only in the highest level of policy and leaves the daily work of the organization to others. Instead, the principals were visible, opened their doors, and were available for spontaneous discussion or problem solving. They spent time with students and tried to be ever-present at school activities, even informal ones. They were in the lunchroom and around the halls not to discipline but to collect information that would help them support teachers' work (Louis and Miles 1990).[13]

Delegating and Empowering. Another quality that these principals shared was promoting conditions that acknowledge teachers' professional capabilities and judgments. Principals who create healthy environments for teachers expect teachers to find solutions to problems. They don't think of themselves as the only problem solvers. The effective principal "can leave the building without things falling apart or hitting snags, and has staff empowered to respond to crises," a teacher remarked. At Hillside, the following comment was typical: "[She] keeps the staff together . . .[;] she does facilitate what we want to do. There are so many things going on in this building that even she admits that she no longer can keep up with what's going on. But what's really neat about [our principal] is that she trusts our professionalism so much that . . . even if she's not aware of every small detail, it's okay."

At all three schools, the philosophical conviction was to empower the group rather than the individual teacher. Communal decisions prevailed, even when administrators were not enthusiastic.

Confronting Unengaged Teachers. Teachers are inspired to work hard by those around them. Over and over again, teachers in these schools stressed the positive impact of a principal's willingness to confront bad teaching. These schools had plenty of supportive strategies to help less effective teachers improve, including mentor teachers; an environment that invited teachers to visit one another's classes; and staff development opportunities.

For example, Brigham's principal worked with several teachers to lessen the amount of lecturing and teacher-centered instruction they did. Ultimately, one teacher left, but others made significant improvements. At City Park, some teachers experienced anxiety about their abilities to advise students in nonacademic matters, but the assistant director put a great deal of personal energy into helping them deal with students more personally. Still, a teacher who was unable to develop supportive relationships with students did not return the next year.

Providing Leadership about Values. Teachers agreed that the principal sets the tone for developing a school's vision and value orientation. It is important for the principal to understand and reflect the best in community ethical standards and values and to "make clear what is valued—don't keep faculty guessing about what is important." Leadership that articulated strong values was most visible at Brigham and City Park, where each principal adhered to a particular educational philosophy. In both cases, the philosophy was based on creating opportunities for collaborative work so that teachers would feel less isolated. In large and well-established Hillside, leadership values played a more subtle role, but teachers still acknowledged them, particularly with regard to increasing parent involvement, developing interdisciplinary curriculums, and caring for students.

A teacher at City Park told us of a visit to her class by a Shakespearean actor: "This guy . . . transformed my class in a way I could never have done. I was overawed by how good he was with my kids. . . . He had one of my kids standing on her head!" Perhaps all of us dream of schools full of such people, but the prospect of transforming schools through exceptional charisma is unrealistic. Such people are rare, and, as this teacher said, "You would run out of them pretty quickly!" Also, even the most talented teachers can burn out if their only support comes from their inner resources.

It is also a mistake to allow teachers to depend only on students as a source of external support and feedback. Doing so puts teachers in frustrating and lonely work environments. At City Park, Brigham, and Hillside, we saw teachers energetically invest in the personal and academic progress of their students. But it was a variety of collegial, administrative, and structural supports helped them remain engaged.

Teachers' engagement with the school as a social unit or community intensifies most profoundly when there is an educational vision. The importance of individual purpose and motivation should not be underestimated. The cases suggest that a supportive culture within a school can compensate significantly for lower demands made by community and parents. Knowledgeable leaders play a pivotal role in establishing such a vision, but planning and decision-making opportunities can quickly involve staff in doing the same.

Engagement with student achievement is nourished by opportunities for teachers to collaborate both on schoolwide decisions and on curriculum and instruction. Too often, collaborative activities converge only on the marginal necessities of school life, such as paperwork, purchasing, or staff parties. At the three schools, teachers as a whole and in smaller groups made decisions about fundamental school issues: the qualities that new teachers should have, student abilities and needs, the nature of teacher-student relationships, the content of the curriculum and the methods of instruction, and the setting or abolishing of policies. Professional dialogue about these tasks builds ownership and empowerment in ways that "zoning of decisions"—in which teachers make individual decisions about how they teach but defer to administrators about policy matters—does not (Johnson 1990). Collaboration also engages teachers with achievement because it provides opportunities for teachers to support and give feedback they may not always get from their students. Finally, opportunities to develop curriculum and instructional plans for their students allows teachers to assess an appropriate level of challenge. This increases the likelihood of students being engaged with their work.

Engagement with students as whole individuals is expedited by structures that allow teachers to interact with students more informally and in smaller groups. In schools where teachers engaged with students, we found a general ethic of care, in addition to structures such as advisory periods. This ethic of care recognizes that students' emotional well being influences their readiness to learn.

Engagement with subject matter took a somewhat different twist in the three schools, as compared with more typical high schools. These schools did not reflect the maxim that "elementary teachers teach students, high school teachers teach subjects." Teachers stayed current with developments in their field by participating in local and national associations, but many also subordinated their own subject specialty to a more interdisciplinary curriculum. The emphasis was on learning together how to best communicate subject matter and working jointly to ensure that subject matter was appropriate and exciting for the kids.

The relationship between teacher engagement and school culture, organization, and leadership is not simple. But the organizational reforms that these schools accomplished demonstrate how schools serving disadvantaged students can sustain levels of teacher engagement comparable to schools in higher socioeconomic circumstances. The success of these three schools is not easy to reproduce. Communities did not pressure these schools to perform; the schools themselves generated high demands for teacher performance and engagement. Teachers in these schools gave themselves freely to the task of instruction and student achievement—but had resources to turn to if classroom success was not immediate or as profound as they hoped. This is, perhaps, the balance to which any restructured school must aspire in order to break the "iron law of social class."

ENDNOTES

1. The research on which the paper is based was supported by the National Center for Effective Secondary Schools, OERI grant G-0086900007.

2. The interconnection between teacher and student engagement and social class is empirically demonstrated in recent qualitative studies (Firestone and Rosenblum 1988, Metz 1990) and those based on large scale data (Dworkin 1987; Brookover et al. 1979; Purkey, Rutter, and Newmann 1987; Bryk, Lee, and Smith 1988; Lee and Smith 1994). See Hurn 1985 for a review of earlier empirical literature. Dworkin (1987), for example, reports that teachers in schools with students from low socioeconomic backgrounds are more likely to be burned out and disengaged, while Purkey, Rutter, and Newmann (1987) show that teachers in urban schools (presumably with higher proportions of children from lower socioeconomic contexts) are less satisfied with their work.

3. This assumption has received strong support in recent analyses. For example, Bryk and Thum (1989) show that schools in which teachers exhibit higher levels of engagement and commitment are less likely to have high rates of student absenteeism and dropouts, while Wehlege and colleagues (1989) provide extensive case studies of programs staffed by engaged teachers, which are highly successful in retaining and improving the achievement of students who are at risk. The "effective schools" research also suggests strong relationships between schoolwide teacher engagement with students and student achievement (Brookover et al. 1979, Wilson and Corcoran 1988).

4. Lee and Smith (1994) demonstrate that teachers' beliefs about their work and students have a strong effect on the equity of students' achievement in high schools.
5. See Metz (1988).
6. This is hardly a novel idea in the general management literature. In his 1938 classic, *The Functions of the Executive*, Chester Barnard counseled top administrators to avoid simplistic ideas about the importance of wages as a motivator and to be aware of the need to create conditions that maximized other incentives, such as the desire for meaningful work, the importance of valued social relationships on the job, and the need for participation. Yet, in education these ideas have rarely been applied to teachers' work and the problems of educational performance.
7. See Bryk and Driscoll 1988, Firestone and Rosenblum 1988, and Wehlege et al. 1989.
8. The research methods used in the study are reported in greater detail in Louis and Smith 1991.
9. Case accounts were completed in all three schools. City Park Secondary School was prepared by Sheila Rosenblum and BetsAnn Smith. Brigham High School was prepared by Stewart Purkey and Karen Seashore Louis. Hillside High School was prepared by Dick Rossmiller and Sheila Rosenblum.
10. Specific survey measures of teacher engagement are available in Louis 1991b.
11. See Mary Metz's research in "typical" high schools, summarized in Louis and Smith 1991.
12. Rossmiller (1992) provides case studies of eight principals located in "traditional high schools" that emphasize the buffering role.
13. See also Louis and Miles (1990). They discuss the importance of "minding the store" in a major change project.

REFERENCES

Barnard, C. (1938). *The Functions of the Executive.* Cambridge, Mass.: Harvard University.

Brookover, W., C. Beady, P. Flood, J. Schweitzer, and J. Wisenbaker. (1979). *School Social Systems and Student Achievement: Schools Can Make a Difference.* New York: Praeger.

Bryk, A.S., and M.W. Driscoll. (1988). *The High School as Community: Contextual Influences and Consequences for Students and Teachers.* Madison, Wisc.: National Center on Effective Secondary Schools, University of Wisconsin-Madison.

Bryk, A.S., J.Q. Easton, D. Kerbow, S.G. Rollow, and P.A. Sebring. (1993). *A View from the Elementary School: The State of Reform in Chicago.* Chicago, Ill.: Consortium on Chicago School Research.

Bryk, A., V. Lee, and J. Smith. (1988). "High School Organization and Its Effects on Teachers and Students: An Interpretive Summary of the Research." In *Choice and Control in Schools,* edited by W. Clune and J. Witte. Philadelphia, Pa.: Falmer.

Bryk, A.S., and Y.M. Thum. (1989). *The Effects of High School Organization on Dropping Out: An Exploratory Investigation.* New Brunswick, N.J.: Center for Policy Research in Education, Rutgers, The State University of New Jersey.

Cibulka, J.G. (1992). "Urban Education as a Field of Study: Problems of Knowledge and Power." In *The Politics of Urban Education in the United States.* Washington, D.C.: Falmer.

Corcoran, T., L. Walker, and J.L. White. (1988). *Working in Urban Schools.* Washington, D.C.: Institute for Educational Leadership.

Corwin, R., and K.S. Louis. (1982). "Organizational Barriers to the Utilization of Research." *Administrative Science Quarterly* 27: 623-640.

Dworkin, A. (1987). *Teacher Burnout in the Public Schools.* Albany, N.Y.: SUNY.

Englert, R. (1993). "Understanding the Urban Context and Conditions of Practice of School Administration." In *City Schools: Leading the Way,* edited by P. Forsyth and M. Tallerico. Newbury Park, Calif.: Corwin.

Firestone, W., and S. Rosenblum. (1988). "The Alienation and Commitment of Students and Teachers in Urban High Schools: A Conceptual Framework." *Educational Evaluation and Policy Quarterly* 10: 285-300.

Freedman, S. (1990). *Small Victories: The Real World of a Teacher, Her Students and Their School.* New York: Harper and Row.

Fuhrman, S. (1993). *Designing Coherent Educational Policy.* San Francisco, Calif.: Jossey-Bass.

Hurn, C. (1985). *The Limits and Possibilities of Schooling.* Boston, Mass.: Allyn and Bacon.

Johnson, S. (1990). "Teachers, Power and School Change." In *Choice and Control in American Education, Vol. 2,* edited by W. Clune and J. Witte. Philadelphia, Pa.: Falmer.

Kidder, T. (1989). *Among School Children.* Boston, Mass.: Houghton Mifflin.

Lee, V., and J. Smith. (1994). "Effects of Restructured Teacher Worklife on Gains in Achievement and Engagement for Early Secondary

School Students." Paper presented at the annual meeting of the American Educational Research Association, New Orleans, La.

Lieberman, A., ed. (1988). *Building a Professional Culture in Schools.* New York: Teachers College.

Louis, K.S. (1991a). "Social and Community Values and the Quality of Teacher Work Life." In *The Context of Teaching in Secondary Schools,* edited by J. Talbert and N. Bascia. Newbury Park, CA: Corwin.

Louis, K.S. (1991b). "Teacher Commitment, Sense of Efficacy and Quality of Work Life: Results from a Survey." Paper presented at the annual meeting of the American Educational Research Association, Chicago, Ill.

Louis, K.S., and M.B. Miles. (1990). *Improving the Urban High School: How it Works.* New York: Teachers College.

Louis, K.S., and B.A. Smith. (1991). "Restructuring, Teacher Engagement and School Culture: Perspectives on School Reform and the Improvement of Teachers' Work." *School Effectiveness and School Improvement* 2: 34-52.

Metz, M.H. (1988). "Teachers' Ultimate Dependence on Their Students: Implications for Teachers' Response to Student Bodies of Differing Social Class." Paper presented at the annual meeting of the American Educational Research Association, New Orleans, La.

Metz, M.H. (1990). "How Social Class Differences Shape the Context of Teachers' Work." In *The Secondary Schools as a Workplace,* edited by M. McLaughlin and J. Talbert. New York: Teachers College.

National Education Association. (1987). *Status of the American Public School Teacher: 1985-1986.* West Haven, Conn.: NEA Professional Library.

Newmann, F.M., ed. (1992). *Student Engagement and Achievement in American Secondary Schools.* New York: Teachers College.

Noddings, N. (1992). *The Challenge to Care in Schools: An Alternative Approach to Education.* New York: Teachers College.

Peterson, P. (1985). *The Politics of School Reform: 1870-1940.* Chicago: University of Chicago.

Purkey, S.C., R.A. Rutter, and F.M. Newmann. (1987). "United States High School Improvement Programs: A Profile from the High School and Beyond Supplemental Survey." *Metropolitan Education* 3: 59-91.

Rollow, S., and A. Bryk. (1995). "Building Professional Community in a School Left Behind by Reform." In *Professionalism and Community: Perspectives on Reforming Urban Schools,* edited by K.S. Louis and S. Kruse. Newbury Park, Calif.: Corwin.

Rossmiller, R. (1992). "The Secondary School Principal and Teachers' Quality of Work Life." *Educational Management and Administration* 20, 3: 132-146.

Senge, P. (1990). *The Fifth Discipline: The Art and Practice of the Learning Organization.* New York: Doubleday.

Wahlberg, H. (1989). "District Size and Learning." *Education and Urban Society* 21: 154-163.

Wehlage, G.G., R.A. Rutter, N.L. Lesko, and R.R. Fernandez. (1989). *Reducing the Risk: Schools as Communities of Support.* Philadelphia, Pa.: Falmer.

Wilson, B., and T. Corcoran. (1988). *Successful Secondary Schools: Visions of Excellence in American Public Schools.* East Sussex, England: Falmer.

8

A Social Vision for Urban Education: Focused, Comprehensive, and Integrated Change

BELINDA WILLIAMS

In the quotation that begins Chapter 1, O'Day and Smith call for a compelling vision of change to improve urban education. This vision should be "powerful enough to focus the public and all levels of the governance system on common challenging purposes and to sustain that focus over an extended period of time" (O'Day and Smith 1993, p. 299). But in order for this vision to come to life, it must be linked to a common set of principles and beliefs held by all segments of our society influencing children's learning, including legislators; teacher educators; teachers; principals; and other school staff, community leaders, parents, and educational researchers.

The authors whose work and ideas appear in this book make two important contributions to shaping a powerful vision of the future for urban schools and communities. First, they define the nature of the achievement gap in urban schools, integrating the knowledge base on human development with what is known about learning in urban contexts. Second, they provide us with a set of guiding principles and strategies for closing that achievement gap. This concluding chapter highlights key ideas contributed by these authors.

NATURE OF THE URBAN ACHIEVEMENT GAP

Strategies for improving urban schools must be grounded in an understanding of the complexities of urban life and the dynamics that have led to poor academic achievement by urban students. Simplistic, reductionist explanations limited to psychological or cognitive perspectives; management solutions; technology; or standards for curriculum, instruction, and assessment fail to consider the interactions and connections between informal (out-of-school) and formal (in-school) learning in urban settings.

The authors in this book clearly agree that urban students' achievement reflects historical, social, and economic events:

• the dynamics of the relocation of industry from cities to the suburbs,

• the transition to a postindustrial service economy,

• the history of racial segregation, and

• a new wave of large-scale immigration.

Together, these events have created the macroecology of urban communities, with concentrations of poverty, cultural diversity, and isolation. Urban schools are caught at the center of these interconnected social problems, daily trying to counteract their effects on children and youth. Benard points out in Chapter 6:

> More than 40 years of social science research clearly identifies poverty as the factor most likely to put an individual at risk of experiencing social problems such as drug abuse, teen pregnancy, child abuse, and violence. Nonetheless, we persist in "blaming the victim" not only for exhibiting the symptoms of poverty but also for the poverty itself (Currie 1993, Polakow 1993, Schor 1992, Wilson 1987). (See Chapter 6.)

In addition, Wang and Kovach note in Chapter 2 that "The more a school draws from poor neighborhoods riddled with social problems, the worse its students perform academically."

The same mix of history and socioeconomics that created the macroecology of urban communities is responsible for the nature of the urban achievement gap. The concentrations of poverty, cultural diversity, and isolation have shaped the knowledge and abilities of urban students and contributed to the mismatch between urban students and schools they attend. This mismatch is the result of what Greenfield, Raeff, and Quiroz see as the difference between the invisible culture of the home and community (social/interpersonal emphasis) and the invisible culture of the school (logical/rational/ individual emphasis).

However, members of the public—as well as some educators themselves—have a vision of the achievement gap that is quite different. Instead of viewing the achievement gap as evolving out of the cultural mismatch cited by the authors, critics have traditionally adhered to a "cultural deficit" perspective that says, in essence, "Urban schools and students can do no better." This misguided perception continues to shape and limit research agendas and policy decisions.

A COMPREHENSIVE SOCIAL VISION FOR URBAN EDUCATION

Urban schools cannot close the gap in students' achievement by themselves. Improvement requires entire communities to get involved. A comprehensive vision for urban schools and communities rests on complex, integrated change in six major areas:

• establishing school-linked services and resources for urban communities and families;

• making urban schools and classrooms culturally compatible with students' home backgrounds and conditions;

• having teachers who communicate high expectations, caring, and cultural sensitivity;

• giving urban students opportunities to learn;

• creating school environments that foster students' resilience; and

• fostering high levels of teacher engagement.

ESTABLISHING SCHOOL-LINKED SERVICES AND RESOURCES FOR URBAN COMMUNITIES AND FAMILIES

Zeichner cautions us that:

Having high expectations for students, cultural congruence in instruction, culturally inclusive curriculum, knowledgeable teachers, and appropriate instructional strategies all contribute to narrowing the achievement gap in urban schools. However, by themselves they are still not enough to overcome the effects of racism, language discrimination, social stratification, unequal resource distribution, and a history of discrimination against poor people of color (Carter and Goodwin 1994, Villegas 1988). (See Chapter 4.)

Wang and Kovach concur with this:

[N]arrowly conceived plans and commitments that focus only on schools will not solve the growing problems that must be addressed to ensure success of the many children and youth who have not fared well under the current system of service delivery. (See Chapter 2)

These authors insist on the creative organization of school-linked community services. They maintain that such services will strengthen families and foster the physical and psychological well-being that lies at the heart of resilience.

Wang and Kovach outline several strategies for establishing school-linked community services:

• Creating broad social policies that enable interagency, collaborative programs to link schools and other service agencies.

• Pooling resources from public and private sectors, such as city and state health and human services departments, businesses, religious institutions, and community-based social and medical service agencies.

• Negotiating new forms of cooperation and coordination, along with new ways of mobilizing community energies and resources.

Further, Wang and Kovach point out that:

[S]ignificant learning occurs outside schools, and the conditions for learning in schools are greatly influenced by the family and all elements of the community. . . .

Despite the difficulties of urban life, cities contain many rich and promising resources for children and families. (See Chapter 2.)

MAKING SCHOOLS AND CLASSROOMS CULTURALLY COMPATIBLE

Greenfield, Raeff, and Quiroz tell us:

> Children come to school acting in accordance with the invisible cultures of their homes and communities. Conflict arises when their behavior differs from the invisible culture of the school. (See Chapter 3.)

They go on to describe the nature of this conflict as emanating from the difference between collectivism, which places high value on interdependence, and the individualism that U.S. schools foster. Further, these authors discuss material and symbolic culture:

> Development and socialization take place as people adapt to different ecological and economic conditions (Berry 1967, 1994; press; Draper and Cashdan 1988). This adaptation accounts for the material side of culture. However, human beings have an intrinsic need to create meaning from their experiences as well (Bruner 1990). How they do so becomes reflected and rationalized in different value orientations. We call this the symbolic side of culture.

Greenfield and her colleagues—Zeichner, Benard, and Wang and Kovach—all cite the need for teachers to become aware of the cultural experiences that their urban students bring to school. In other words, they should be aware of what these students know and are able to do and the meanings they attach to their ecological conditions.

HAVING TEACHERS WHO COMMUNICATE HIGH EXPECTATIONS, CARING, AND CULTURAL SENSITIVITY

Zeichner observes:

> In culturally congruent classrooms, students can apply language and task completion skills that are already in their repertoires.

> Teachers can, however, incorporate culture and language-sensitive practices into instruction in their classrooms so that

students feel there is respect for their cultural roots.
(See Chapter 4 for sources of Zeichner's observations.)

Zeichner summarizes four key elements concerning what teachers need to be like, to know, and to be able to do to teach all students to high academic standards:

• Teachers need to have high expectations, to believe that all students can succeed, and to communicate this belief to their students.

• Teachers need to build cultural congruence into instruction, bridging students' knowledge, cultural traditions, and languages with the school culture while at the same time explicitly teaching the codes and customs of the school.

• Teachers need knowledge about sociocultural development and second language acquisition, as well as knowledge about the circumstances of students in their classrooms. They also need knowledge of their own ethnic and cultural identities.

• Teachers need instructional strategies that focus on "meaning making" and reciprocal instruction methods (guidance and facilitation).

These four elements imply serious change for teacher preparation. Zeichner proposes two new requirements for teacher education institutions: (1) screening to ensure that all prospective teachers have a commitment to teaching all students to high academic standards; and (2) programs to develop cultural sensitivity and intercultural teaching competence. He cautions against cultural stereotyping and recommends that preservice and inservice programs assist teachers in acquiring strategies for obtaining and incorporating into their instruction information about their students, their families, and their communities. Such strategies may include visiting homes; conferring with community members; talking with students, parents, and minority teachers; and observing students in and out of school.

GIVING URBAN STUDENTS OPPORTUNITIES TO LEARN

In order for urban students to achieve the standards established for all students, schools must eliminate assessment procedures that produce disproportionate labeling (tracking, remediation, special education). Disproportionate labeling dampens the expectations of both teachers and students and limits students' exposure to curriculum and instruction.

Stevens strongly recommends four standards to ensure that schools give all students an opportunity to learn. These standards focus on content coverage, content exposure, content emphasis, and quality of instructional delivery. She cautions:

> Observers who attribute minority students' low achievement solely to society's ills tend to dismiss the very important influences of schools and teachers in student learning.

> Opportunity to learn is a key factor in children's learning—perhaps the most critical one. (See Chapter 5.)

In addition, she describes the kind of family support that encourages students' academic achievement, the management of the school environment so that students can meet performance and behavior standards, and the assessment of students' academic achievement. Stevens' strategies for assessing and measuring whether schools are truly giving students an opportunity to learn include using teacher logs, observations, surveys, interval testing, and small assessment tasks. She concludes that:

> Opportunity to learn changes the way we look at student outcome data. Just as the international studies . . . looked beyond race, SES, and gender to the instructional and cultural practices in different countries, we must do the same when looking at different groups of students in the United States. (See Chapter 5.)

CREATING SCHOOL ENVIRONMENTS THAT FOSTER STUDENTS' RESILIENCE

Benard outlines ways for schools to increase opportunities for students to develop resilience. The protective factors that foster resiliency in children and diminish the effects of abuse, crime, drugs, and poverty are lodged in caring and supportive environments where teachers communicate high expectations and students have many opportunities to participate in making decisions about their learning. As Benard states: "[P]rotective factors . . . enable individuals to circumvent life stresses." (See Chapter 6.)

The traits that contribute to individual resiliency are in four broad categories: social competence, problem-solving skills, autonomy, and a sense of purpose and future. Teachers can foster all of these through instruction that incorporates cooperative learning, builds on student knowledge and abilities, makes learning tasks meaningful, introduces formal curriculum content with an eye toward community issues and student experiences, and connects learning to students' images of their future.

FOSTERING HIGH LEVELS OF TEACHER ENGAGEMENT

If schools are to provide culturally responsive instruction, enhance resilience, and give all students an opportunity to learn, what is required of teachers who serve urban populations? Louis and Smith cite research on organizational conditions that facilitate teacher engagement and enable teachers to experience success with students. They describe four types of teacher engagement: two are affective and focus on human relationships, and two are instrumental and focus on the goals of teaching and learning.

In the area of the affective:

• Teachers engage with the school as a social unit, and there is community and personal caring among adults as well as integration between personal and work life.

• Teachers engage with students as unique, whole individuals and respond to students' personal and school lives.

In the area of the instrumental:

• Teachers engage with academic achievement, developing and sharing curriculum and assessment ideas and experiences.

• Teachers engage with a body of knowledge, keeping sharp their knowledge of content and ways to connect that content to students' lives.

Also according to Louis and Smith, several conditions are necessary in a school in order for teacher engagement to take place. Among those conditions:

• The school culture instills a clear sense of mission, closeness among staff, respect and caring for students, active problem solving among teachers, and peer pressure to work.

• The school organization reinforces the staff's commitment to teaching.
• The school leadership supports teachers.

Louis and Smith conclude:

> Teachers in these schools gave themselves freely to the task of instruction and student achievement—but had resources to turn to if classroom success was not immediate or as profound as they hoped. This is, perhaps, the balance to which any restructured school must aspire in order to break the "iron law of social class." (See Chapter 7.)

GUIDING PRINCIPLES AND STRATEGIES TO ACHIEVE THIS VISION FOR URBAN SOCIAL AND EDUCATIONAL CHANGE

The research on human development and learning cited by these authors and the social vision they have collectively created have implications for each segment of the educational community involved in reform initiatives.

Legislators who are responsible for policies and resource allocations must focus on:

• Alignment of federal, state, and community policies, and creation of new legislation that recognizes, and is sensitive to, the macroecological dynamics that affect urban communities, families, students, and schools. They also must provide the resources to support families, students, and schools.

• Collaboration among different agencies to ensure caring community, home, and school environments and a sense of a positive future.

• Identification of and legislative support for alternatives to segregating students according to race, ethnicity, socioeconomics, and ability.

• Comprehensive, long-range planning that minimizes fragmentation and reductionist strategies that are limited to curriculum and assessment standards and decentralization.

Teacher preparation institutions must look to:
• Professional development programs that integrate the disciplines of psychology, sociology, and cultural anthropology and increase the valuing and understanding of human development and learning in urban contexts (e.g., effects of culture and poverty on the acquisition of knowledge and skills).
• Criteria to screen into teaching those people who have a commitment to teach all students.
• Program content and field experiences that increase the understanding and impact of culture on students' personal development.
• Increased understanding of the impact of teachers' own culture on their personal development.
• Strategies for acquiring information about the cultural community, family, and student knowledge along with students' activities and abilities.
• Strategies for developing connections between students' experiences, knowledge, and abilities and formal curriculum and assessment standards.
• Strategies for developing higher-order thinking abilities through meaningful, authentic presentations of the formal curriculum.
• Increased faculty involvement in urban schools and communities.

Educators in general must focus on:
• Increased and ongoing time for professional development, planning, collaboration, and collegial support.
• Increased understanding that students must "attach and bond" to people and programs in schools in order to learn.
• Development of authentic curriculums, instruction, and assessment that are relevant to the lives, experiences, and futures of students.
• Programming that ensures inclusion and opportunity to learn, content coverage, content exposure, content emphasis, and quality instruction.
• Instructional strategies that stress simultaneous promotion of students' home and community cultures and accommodation to the mainstream culture.

• Project- or task-focused heterogeneous ability grouping, peer tutoring, and cooperative learning activities.

• Explicit instruction that communicates the codes and customs of schools ("codes of power").

• Introduction of community related themes and interaction patterns into the school and classroom.

• Instruction that communicates a belief that all students can succeed.

• Instruction and school environments that communicate caring and concern for students.

• Reciprocal instruction that includes student-selected themes and academic tasks that are relevant to students' lives.

Community leaders and parents must attend to:

• Integrated support services and caring for families and students.

• Identification and integration of social and community issues with instruction.

• Identification and integration of community resources—including resources from the professional and business community—with instructional projects and activities.

• Community service projects for students.

• Meaningful parental involvement in school activities.

• Opportunities for parents to develop skills and a sense of future.

Educational researchers must consider:

• Development of cross-disciplinary theories of human development and learning specific to the urban context.

• Exploration of strategies for changing teacher belief systems and the perception of student differences as deficits or fixed abilities.

• Attention to unanswered questions such as: How does the concentration of poverty, diversity, and isolation affect learning? What abilities are developed in the urban context? How can instruction connect the urban experience and the meanings of formal curriculums? How do the different values cultures place on cognitive and social development influence learning?

The vision for urban educational change that the authors in this book present is clear. For urban schools to successfully educate urban children, we must have coordinated social support for urban communities, families, and students as well as integrated, culturally responsive school programs. The entire educational community needs to work together in reviewing existing and proposed programs and policies in light of these recommendations and in expanding, revising, or eliminating them as necessary. Everyone who has an opportunity to address these critical reform challenges has the chance to make an important contribution to the lives of poor urban children and the society in which we all live.

We close with some final thoughts about this vision for urban education. Wang and Kovach suggest:

> If only we can find the means of magnifying the "positives" in urban life, we can rekindle hope for improving our capacity for education in urban communities. (See Chapter 2.)

Benard concludes that, "[F]ostering resiliency in urban schools requires working politically for educational, social, and economic justice." (See Chapter 6.) She quotes Alex Molnar (1994), professor of Education at the University of Wisconsin-Milwaukee, who says:

> At their heart. . .the problems of city schools are the result of our failure to place school reform inside of a broader vision of social and economic justice and our unwillingness to engage in the kind of political activity necessary to realize that vision (p. 59).

REFERENCES

Berry, J.W. (1967). "Independence and Conformity in Subsistence-Level Societies." *Journal of Personality and Social Psychology* 7, 4: 415-418.

Bruner, J.S. (1990). *Acts of Meaning.* Cambridge, Mass.: Harvard University.

Carter, R.T., and A.L. Goodwin. (1994). "Racial Identity and Education." In *Review of Research in Education, 20,* edited by L. Darling-Hammond. Washington, D.C.: American Educational Research Association.

Currie, E. (1993). *Reckoning: Drugs, the Cities, and the American Future.* New York: Hill and Wang.

Draper, P., and E. Cashdan. (1988). "Technological Change and Child Behavior Among the !Kung." *Ethnology* 27: 339-365.

Molnar, A. (1994). "City Schools Under Attack." *Educational Leadership* 51, 8: 58-59.

O'Day, J.A., and M.S. Smith. (1993). "Systemic Reform and Educational Opportunity." In *Designing Coherent Education Policy: Improving the System*, edited by S.H. Fuhrman. San Francisco, Calif.: Jossey-Bass.

Polakow, V. (1993). *Lives on the Edge: Single Mothers and Their Children in the Other America*. Chicago, Ill.: University of Chicago.

Schor, J. (1992). *The Overworked American: The Unexpected Decline of Leisure*. New York: Basic Books.

Villegas, A.M. (1988). "School Failures and Cultural Mismatch: Another View." *The Urban Review* 20, 4: 253-265.

Wilson, W.J. (1987). *The Truly Disadvantaged: The Inner City, the Underclass, and Public Policy*. Chicago: University of Chicago.

Appendix
Regional Educational Laboratories

Appalachia Educational Laboratory (AEL)
P.O. Box 1348
Charleston, WV 25325
Tel.: (304) 347-0400
Fax: (304) 347-0487
Director: Terry L. Eidell
(Region Served: Kentucky, Tennessee, Virginia, and West Virginia)

The Laboratory for Student Success (LSS)
Temple University
933 Ritter Hall Annex
Philadelphia, PA 19122
Tel.: (215) 204-3001
Fax: (215) 204-5130
Director: Margaret C. Wang
(Region Served: Delaware, Maryland, New Jersey, Pennsylvania, and District of Columbia)

Mid-Continent Regional Educational Laboratory (McREL)
2550 S. Parker Rd., Ste. 500
Aurora, CO 80014
Tel.: (303) 337-0990
Fax: (303) 337-3005
Director: Timothy Waters
(Region Served: Colorado, Kansas, Nebraska, Missouri, Wyoming, North Dakota, and South Dakota)

North Central Regional Educational Laboratory (NCREL)
1900 Spring Rd., Ste. 300
Oak Brook, IL 60521
Tel.: (708) 571-4700
Fax: (708) 571-4716
Director: Jeri Nowakowski
(Region Served: Illinois, Indiana, Iowa, Michigan, Minnesota, Ohio, and Wisconsin)

Northeast and Islands Regional Educational Laboratory at Brown University (LAB)
222 Richmond St.
Providence, RI 02906-4384
Tel.: (401) 274-9548
Fax: (401) 421-7650
Director: Mary Lee Fitzgerald
(Region Served: Connecticut, Maine, Massachusetts, New Hampshire, New York, Rhode Island, Vermont, Puerto Rico, and the Virgin Islands)

Northwest Regional Educational Laboratory (NWREL)
101 S.W. Main St., Ste. 500
Portland, OR 97204
Tel.: (503) 275-9500
Fax: (503) 275-9489
Director: Ethel Simon McWilliams
(Region Served: Alaska, Idaho, Oregon, Montana, and Washington)

Pacific Region Educational Laboratory (PREL)
828 Fort Street Mall, Ste. 500
Honolulu, HI 96813
Tel.: (808) 533-6000
Fax: (808) 533-7599
Director: John W. Kofel
(Region Served: American Samoa, Commonwealth of the Northern Mariana Islands, Federated States of Micronesia, Guam, Hawaii, Republic of the Marshall Islands, and Republic of Palau)

SouthEastern Regional Vision for Education (SERVE)
University of North Carolina at Greensboro
P.O. Box 5367
Greensboro, NC 27435
Tel.: (910) 334-3211
Fax: (910) 334-3268
Director: Roy H. Forbes
(Region Served: Alabama, Florida, Georgia, Mississippi, North Carolina, and South Carolina)

Southwest Educational Development Laboratory (SEDL)
211 E. Seventh St.
Austin, TX 78701
Tel.: (512) 476-6861
Fax: (512) 476-2286
Director: Preston C. Kronkosky
(Region Served: Arkansas, Louisiana, New Mexico, Oklahoma, and Texas)

WestEd Laboratory for Educational Research and Development (WestEd)
730 Harrison St.
San Francisco, CA 94107
Tel.: (415) 565-3000
Fax: (415) 565-3012
Director: Dean H. Nafziger
(Region Served: Arizona, California, Nevada, and Utah)

ABOUT THE AUTHORS

Bonnie Benard

Bonnie Benard holds a Masters of Social Work from the University of Missouri at Columbia. She has been a Prevention Specialist at the Western Center for Drug-Free Schools and Communities, Far West Laboratory for Educational Research and Development. She writes articles for publication, presents workshops on prevention policy and programming, consults with various state and national organizations, and serves on the advisory boards of several national prevention projects. She is especially well-known for her work on fostering resiliency in students. During the last decade, Benard has written frequently about effective prevention strategies and programs. Address: Resiliency Associates, P.O. Box 105, 1678 Shattuck Ave., Berkeley, CA 94709. Tel.: (510) 433-7188

Patricia Marks Greenfield

Patricia Marks Greenfield received her Ph.D. from Harvard University, and her distinguished career in developmental psychology spans three decades. Currently Professor of Psychology at the University of California at Los Angeles, she is internationally known for her work, which focuses on the influence of culture on language development and cognitive growth and the effect of video games, computers, and television on learning. Greenfield has received numerous awards for both her teaching and research. Among them are the 1992 American Association for the Advancement of Science Prize for Behavioral Research and the 1992 Distinguished Teaching Award from the American Psychological Association. Throughout her career she has been active professionally by serving on committees and advisory boards, making presentations at professional meetings in the U.S. and abroad, and writing numerous articles and books, many of which have been translated into foreign languages. Address: Department of Psychology, UCLA, Los Angeles, 90095-1563. Tel.: (310) 825-7526. E-mail: greenfie@psych.sscnet.ucla.edu.

John A. Kovach

John A. Kovach is an Assistant Professor of Sociology at Penn State University and currently serves as Director of Outreach and Dissemination at the Temple University Center for Research in Human Development and Education. He has both research and applied experience related to educational programming and evaluation in minority and adult education. He has been a Senior Research Associate with the Adult Learning Project in Washington, D.C.; has directed the National Indian

Adult Education Needs Survey for the Office of Indian Education; and has written articles and book chapters dealing with poverty and education, Native American education policy, and adolescent drug use. His current research focuses on education policy and the sociology of downward mobility. Address: Pennsylvania State University, Delaware County Campus, Media, PA 19063. E-mail: JAK23@psuvm.psu.edu

Karen Seashore Louis

Karen Seashore Louis has been Professor of Educational Policy and Administration in the College of Education and Human Development at the University of Minnesota since 1987 and is currently Associate Dean for Academic Affairs. Her doctorate in sociology was earned at Columbia University, and her major areas of specialization include: organizational behavior, knowledge utilization, sociology of education, and research methods and evaluation research. Recent writing and research explore the topics of school improvement and change, quality of teacher work life, professional socialization and ethics in graduate school, and academic-industry relations in science. Louis is also active in comparative studies of educational systems and was a Fulbright Scholar in the Netherlands in 1995-96. Address: University of Minnesota, 104 Burton Hall, 178 Pillsbury Drive S.E., Minneapolis, MN 55455. Tel.: (612) 625-6806.

Blanca Quiroz

Blanca Quiroz recently completed two years as a bilingual kindergarten and 1st-grade teacher in Los Angeles. She received her B.A. in psychology from the University of California at Los Angeles (UCLA) in 1993. While at UCLA she held both research and field-work assistantships within the Department of Psychology. She received the Psychology Minority Undergraduate Research Award from the UCLA Department of Psychology and the Center for Academic Research Excellence award from the UCLA Division of Life Sciences. She is bilingual and bicultural: a Spanish and English reader, writer, and speaker. Address: Latin American Studies Room 10347 Bunche Hall, UCLA, Los Angeles, CA 90095. Tel.: (310) 206-9046.

Catherine Raeff

Catherine Raeff is currently Assistant Professor of Psychology at Indiana University of Pennsylvania. She held a Post Doctoral Research Fellowship in Applied Developmental Studies from 1993-95, and also taught at the University of California at Los Angeles (UCLA). She received her Ph.D. from Clark University in 1993 and was both a teaching and research assistant while pursuing graduate studies. Raeff's research focuses on parenting, mother-child interaction, and cultural conflict in the classroom and between home and school. She served as coprincipal investigator of two research studies with Patricia Marks Greenfield at UCLA. She has published articles related to her research. Address: Psychology Department, Indiana University of Pennsylvania, Indiana, PA 15701. Tel.: (412) 357-2422.

BetsAnn Smith

BetsAnn Smith received her Ph.D. in Educational Policy and Administration from the University of Minnesota. Her research has examined how changes to school organizations and the teaching profession improve urban schools. Smith worked for the National Center for Effective Secondary Schools and the Center for School Organization and Restructuring before taking her current position as a Research Project Director at the Consortium for Chicago School Research at the University of Chicago. Address: Consortium on Chicago School Research, 1313 E. 60th Street, Chicago, IL 60637. Tel.: (312) 702-4473. Fax: (312) 702-2010.

Floraline Ingram Stevens

Floraline Ingram Stevens is currently an independent evaluation consultant after retiring from the Los Angeles Unified School District in June 1994. Prior to her present position, she served from 1992-94 as a Program Director at the National Science Foundation in the Division of Research, Evaluation, and Dissemination, Directorate for Education and Human Resources. She continues to work with the National Science Foundation as an expert working with the meta-evaluation of the Ventures in Education Program and the project evaluation workshops being held throughout the United States. As a Senior Fellow at the National Center for Education Statistics, she researched the topic of opportunity to learn in relation to equity for poor and minority students and has had research published on the topic by the Office of Educational Research and Improvement (OERI) and the *Journal of Negro Education*. Before her positions at the national level, she held long-term tenure with the Los Angeles Unified School District as Director of the Program Evaluation and Assessment Branch. Stevens is active professionally on several national advisory boards of educational institutions, projects, associations, and publications. Her doctorate, earned at the University of California at Los Angeles, is in the field of Educational Psychology, Educational Research and Evaluation. Address: 4430 Cromwell Ave., Los Angeles, CA 90027. Tel.: (213) 664-0631.

Margaret C. Wang
Margaret C. Wang is Professor of Educational Psychology and the founder and current Director of the Temple University Center for Research in Human Development and Education, which is a broad-based interdisciplinary research and development center focusing on the human development and education related fields. She also serves as the Executive Director of the Mid-Atlantic Laboratory for Student Success, which is one of ten regional education laboratories funded by the U.S. Department of Education, as well as the Director of the National Center on Education in the Inner Cities, a research and development center established by the Office of Educational Research and Improvement of the U.S. Department of Education. Wang is recognized nationally and internationally for her research on learner differences and classroom learning, student motivation, and implementation and evaluation of innovative school programs that are responsive to student diversity. She is the developer of two major school programs: the Primary Education Program and the Adaptive Learning Environments Model. She is the author of 11 books and more than 100 articles and chapters in a variety of researcher- and practitioner-oriented journals and books. She has received numerous awards including the Spencer Fellowship of the National Academy of Education, and she is a fellow of the Division of Educational Psychology and the Division of Child, Youth and Family Services of the American Psychological Association. Address: Temple University, 933 Ritter Hall Annex, Philadelphia, PA 19122. Tel.: (215) 204-3001.

Belinda Williams
Belinda Williams is currently Program Development Specialist for Northeast and Islands Regional Educational Laboratory at Brown University and consultant, Urban Education Associates. Williams received her doctorate in psychology from Rutgers University and has more than 20 years experience studying the academic achievement patterns of culturally different and poor students in urban districts. Her experiences and research have specifically focused on the influence of cultural environments on learning and the implications for curriculum, instruction, assessment, and staff development. For several years she held the position of Director of the Urban Education Project at Research for Better Schools (RBS). The project was responsible for conducting research, development, and technical assistance activities relating to the improvement and restructuring of urban school districts in the Mid-Atlantic region. Before her appointment at RBS, Williams was employed by the Paterson, N.J., public schools for 17 years as Special Assistant to the Superintendent, Director of Research and Development, and Affirmative

Action Officer. Her recent work and publications focus on the impact of cultural differences on the cognitive development and learning of poor children. Williams received the 1993 Ida B. Wells Award from the National Alliance of Black School Educators. Address: Northeast and Islands Regional Educational Laboratory at Brown University, 222 Richmond St., Providence, RI 02906-4384. Tel.: (401) 274-9548.

Kenneth M. Zeichner

Kenneth M. Zeichner, who holds a doctorate in school organizational behavior and change from Syracuse University, has been active as a teacher educator for more than 20 years. In his current position of Professor in the Department of Curriculum and Instruction at the University of Wisconsin-Madison, Zeichner teaches at both the graduate and undergraduate levels and is active in sharing his expertise with professional organizations, the university, and the greater community by working with various committees and study groups and by making presentations. Throughout his career, Zeichner has written extensively on teacher socialization and development. Recent publication topics include preparing teachers for cultural diversity, action research, and reflective teaching. He was recipient of the 1993 Award for Excellence in Professional Writing from the Association of Colleges of Teacher Education and is currently Vice President of the Division of Teaching and Teacher Education in the American Educational Research Association. Address: Wisconsin Center for Education Research, 225 N. Mills St., Madison, WI 53706. Tel.: (608) 263-4651.